The New Cranks Recipe Book

Text © Cranks Retail Ltd, 1996
Colour photographs © Gus Filgate, 1996

Cranks Retail Ltd has asserted its moral right to
be to be identified as the Author of this Work

First published in 1996
by George Weidenfeld & Nicolson Ltd

This paperback edition first published in 1997 by
Phoenix Illustrated
Orion Publishing Group, Orion House
5, Upper St. Martin's Lane
London WC2H 9EA

British Library Cataloguing-in-Publication Data
A catalogue record for this book is available from
the British Library

ISBN 0-75380-037-3

Designed by Bridgewater Books
Edited by Gillian Haslam
Black & white photography by Phil Starling
Styling by Penny Markham
Home Economy by Louise Pickford

The New Cranks Recipe Book

NADINE ABENSUR

PHOENIX ILLUSTRATED

contents

Vegetarian food has been at the heart of a culinary revolution in the past five years. The driving force behind this change is a public that is less rigidly attached to a mode of eating that centres around meat. A more health-conscious and cosmopolitan attitude now informs the eating habits of the population and the influence of other continents; Asia and the Middle East as well as the cooking of the Mediterranean have had much to do with this.

In the cooking of all these cultures, vegetables play a vital role and a meal is quite commonly composed of several smaller courses, giving wider scope for imaginative use of ingredients, notably vegetables. With the increase in travel abroad has come a greater openness to external influences. Until very recent years, supermarkets offered no more than basics. Fresh food sections were rather miserable affairs and local grocers, while offering fresh produce, stocked only a limited range.

uction

Now travel and cookery writers, television programmes devoted to gastronomy and food magazines with vast circulations are helping to make food exciting and fashionable. The British public, after years in the wilderness, is experiencing food and cooking in a totally different way. They have seen and tasted and now want to do it for themselves. Cookery books are selling in unprecedented numbers and it is the new-found appreciation of vegetables that is the key

to making modern cookery a fresh and lively art. It is as if we are waking from a deep sleep and are seeing for the first time a rainbow-coloured display of vegetables. Nightmare memories of overboiled potatoes and soggy greens are finally retreating to the hinterland where they belong.

Supermarkets buy up entire fields to grow crops at home and abroad. Some food enthusiasts argue in favour of home-grown produce and seasonality, yet we hunger for variety and for the produce which we in climatically challenged Britain must seek from sunnier climes. The seasonality question will continue to be debated. But having acquired a taste for the exotic, we are not likely to hurry back to seasonal rationing. We will experiment with vegetables that look as if they come from another planet, with tastes that would have frightened us not so long ago.

More people are going on cookery courses, eager to acquire the skills which were lost as long ago as our grandmother's generation. An increasing number are now far more aware of what they eat and its effect on their health. More fruit and vegetables are seen as essential for a healthy diet. And there is increasing discomfort about modern animal husbandry, with the factory rearing of livestock. As a result we are being more adventurous and replacing more of our meals with vegetarian options.

So there could not be a better time to bring out a new Cranks recipe book. In here you will find dozens of ways to prepare vegetarian meals: some are very simple and others more sophisticated. In the chapter on main courses, you will find the simpler recipes at the beginning and the more sophisticated ones further on. You will discover new combinations and seasonings and we hope you will be inspired to create some concoctions of your own.

For over 35 years Cranks has been the leader in changing Britain's views on vegetarian food and its story in many ways reflects the prevailing culture of the times.

Cranks, in the early sixties, was not only at the centre of burgeoning new values, it helped to establish them. Founded by husband and wife team David and Kay Canter and their friend Daphne Swann, Cranks quickly became known for its radical approach to food and service and its then highly unusual interiors. Against an English culinary background, only just out of the fifties and with rationing still fresh in the memory, the attitudes of David, Kay and Daphne were little short of revolutionary. To a public for whom the word salad meant nothing else than limp lettuce, thick-skinned cucumber and under-ripe tomatoes perhaps dresssed in a rather horrible concoction called salad-cream, if dressed at all, the team introduced bowlfuls of colourful, fresh vegetables, artfully combined and thoughtfully dressed. The look was abundant and alive.

The first Cranks restaurant opened in Carnaby Street, then London's most swinging street. With an ardour, bordering on the zealous, the team took on ever greater challenges. They sourced organically grown, stone-ground flours and against difficult odds used organically grown vegetables whenever possible. They searched for and found someone who would produce additive-free yoghurt and ice cream.

Based on this philosophy Cranks expanded in the seventies and eighties to a chain of ten restaurants and had a number of owners who had identified its appeal.

Meanwhile a revolution was taking place in the food world – new kitchen and diet aesthetics were being formed.

Food was becoming lighter and more delicate, and in

the philo

contrast, the vegetarian food on offer could seem very dull, heavy and – more than anything – brown. In addition there began the extraordinary influence of what has become known as the 'Mediterranean Diet', a diet rich in vegetables and polyunsaturated fats. Every supermarket in the country now boasts several types of olive oil and stocks all year round numerous vegetables and fruits hitherto unknown or forgotten. Whatever anyone may thing of this, there can be no argument over the increased sophistication and demands of the general public and their much greater receptivity to foods that are seen firstly as delicious, and then as vegetarian.

At the same time, large numbers of people began to look critically at their diet, realizing that this is one of the most important ingredients for good health. The Department of Health has helped in pushing this idea through their 'Balance of Good Health' initiative. No longer are calorie-controlled or low-fat diets limited to the fanatical few and the need to eat more fruit and vegetables in one's daily diet has become common knowledge.

A new public has emerged and is making increasing demands on vegetarian cooking. Once regarded as cranky – hence the name – vegetarian food is now becoming accepted as mainstream. Indeed it has become one of the fastest-growing food sectors in the country. Enormous advances have been made in the approach to vegetarian cookery. Vegetables, the poor relative, have taken centre stage.

Cranks, for so much of its thirty years far ahead of its time, had by the early nineties fallen behind these trends. The concept that had seemed so avant garde, now seemed outdated.

The interiors which had once captured the imagination of a generation now seemed trapped in a time warp, and the company began to experience financial difficulties as a result. By 1992 the company had been sold to a combination of existing managers and Piper Trust, a firm specializing in retail development. With new funding, enormous enthusiasm and renewed vision, the team set about the company's rejuvenation.

Cranks' new management quickly saw the menu's relaunch as an absolute necessity to satisfy the new generation's discerning and internationally educated taste buds, whilst still offering value for money. As much as possible the new menu adheres to the core values that were introduced by David Canter. We are still passionate about providing delicious, healthy, vegetarian food. Unless costs are prohibitive or the taste suffers, we use as natural ingredients as possible; they are always additive-free, and always vegetarian. We are now using white, unbleached flour, but this is still organic and is appropriate for the success of certain recipes, but our eggs remain free-range.

With the new menu came many changes. Improbable combinations such as lentil lasagnes have been replaced with altogether lighter, brighter alternatives. Where once there had been a perceived need to replace or imitate meat, vegetables are now used with no apologies. The menu still consists of some of the old favourites. Homity Pie is still on the menu after 35 years; there was such an outcry in the weeks when alternatives were proposed and, besides, it is delicious. But nowadays, side by side with it may appear Polenta with Roasted Vegetables or Pasta with Sundried Tomatoes, Broccoli and Black Olives or Noodles with Pumpkin and Coriander in a Coconut Sauce. Next to the flapjacks may sit a Pear and Almond Tart, and next to the legendary Carrot Cake, a Lemon Tart made with oodles of double cream. You can eat as healthily or as decadently as you wish.

So Cranks in the nineties is alive and kicking. More than

ever, we are committed to providing delicious, healthy, vegetarian food. More than anything we want our food to be relevant and available every day to the many, not the few. The recipes in this book demonstrate how Cranks has updated itself to the new generation. The best of the old sit side by side with the new, just as they do in our restaurants.

Our existing branches provide us with a limited coverage (all but one in London), but all have been recently refurbished and each has a distinct character reflecting its location. St Christopher's Place with its fashionable shops can seem smart and sophisticated. Our Covent Garden branch, in one of London's busiest shopping tourist spots, is always packed and its large outside seating area on the Piazza makes it a major attraction, especially in the summer. Adelaide Street, near Charing Cross, inevitably acts as a godsend to weary commuters. Great Newport Street is an arty place, in the heart of theatreland, and Marshall Street with its unique role as oldest branch and so close to Soho and a rejuvenated Carnaby Street attracts many famous faces. Tottenham Street is an oasis of a restaurant with a stunning glass roof which lets in masses of natural light. Our Dartington branch in Devon, recently refurbished and part of a thriving Arts and Crafts centre, attracts hungry visitors by the coachload. In addition Culinary Arts from Cranks offers delicious and elegant vegetarian food for all corporate and private functions. And in our attempt to make our products as widely available as possible, Cranks Cuisine is developing its own range of ready-made meals and offer products that will be available nationwide to the catering trade and will be introduced slowly into major supermarkets.

Our public is demanding more options in terms of taste and health, convenience and value. We look forward to meeting these challenges, and to maintaining our place at the forefront of healthy eating well into the 21st century.

starters

A starter is quite literally an entry into a meal. It calms the hunger and whets the appetite. In this chapter, the recipes range from an elegant Feta cheese soufflé with sundried tomato purée to a robust Spanish omelette.

It is virtually impossible to plate a main course for more than one or two people without assistance or without ending up with cold food, but this first course is a completely different story. A cold starter can be plated in advance, made to look picture perfect and still allow you time to be with your guests.

Soups and salads make perfect starters as do many of the vegetable dishes from the vegetable and side dishes chapter. Some of the recipes in this section are also ideal as main courses for lighter or summer meals. The rice-based recipes can all be made as individual timbales and served with a sauce or salsa. In fact, many of the savoury recipes in this book can be adapted, by being served in smaller portions. So, when you have exhausted the recipes in this section, scour the other chapters for inspiration.

SPANISH POTATO OMELETTE

Spanish omelette, or at least a version of it, was a common meal in my childhood. It tended to have more vegetables than the recipe given here and was baked in the oven. However, many years ago on a summer holiday to Cadaques in northern Spain, I witnessed the cooking of a dish which made me want to cook for the first time. While the rest of us impoverished foreign students ate from the campsite's none too promising facilities, the Spanish students were well equipped with their Calor gas stoves, their eggs and potatoes, their tomatoes and olive oil and even their strings of garlic. And in front of our jealous eyes, they cooked a Spanish omelette like this (or as similar to this as I remember) every day.

INGREDIENTS

SERVES
4 – 6

- 200 ml / 8 fl oz light olive oil or a mixture of olive and sunflower oil
- 3 medium potatoes, peeled and thinly sliced
- 1 large onion, thinly sliced or diced
- 1 or more cloves of garlic, crushed
- 8 eggs, size 3, lightly beaten
- 3–4 tomatoes, diced
- salt and freshly ground black pepper

METHOD

Pour a little under half the olive oil into a large heavy-based frying pan. Add all the potato and onion, salt and pepper and the crushed garlic and cover with the rest of the oil. Cover with a lid and simmer very gently over a low flame until the vegetables are tender. This will take at least half an hour. Don't allow the vegetables to brown in the slightest – the potatoes should be meltingly tender and quite waxy. Lift out with a kitchen spoon and drain on kitchen paper, reserving the oil. Then beat the eggs and add the potatoes to them. Heat 3 tbsp of the reserved oil and return to the frying pan on a medium heat. Tip in the chopped tomatoes and then the egg and potato mixture.

Cook until three-quarters set. The sides will go a rich golden brown. If you have a grill, finish by browning the omelette under it. If not, cook a little longer in the pan. Allow to cool for a few minutes and turn out. Eat hot or cold.

MANGO, PAPAYA AND AVOCADO SALAD

WITH CRUMBLED DOLCELATTE
AND ORANGE AND RASPBERRY DRESSING

I particularly enjoy food which balances the five tastes – sweet, salt, bitter, hot, sour. This salad should, of course, be eaten in the tropics but spoilt as we are, we may enjoy it in the warmth of an English summer's day. Use the very best fruit you can find.

SERVES
2 – 4

INGREDIENTS

- 1 fragrant mango
- 1 ripe papaya
- 1 Hass avocado
- 100 g / 4 oz pineapple
- 1 scant handful fresh coriander
- 50 g / 2 oz raspberries, reserving 5–6 to crush into the dressing
- 50 g / 2 oz Dolcelatte, Gorgonzola or other mild, creamy blue-veined cheese, crumbled

- 50g / 2 oz blueberries
- 50 g / 2 oz shelled walnuts, preferably fresh
- freshly ground black pepper

FOR THE DRESSING

- 2 tbsp olive oil or walnut oil
- 200 ml / 8 fl oz fresh orange juice
- 1 heaped tsp grain mustard

METHOD

Cut the mango, papaya, avocado and pineapple into even-sized cubes and mix together with the coriander and black pepper. Mix the dressing ingredients together with the reserved raspberries and add to the salad. Scatter the cheese, raspberries, blueberries and walnuts on top and serve at once.

AUBERGINE AND WILD RICE GATEAU

Pasta, potatoes, rice; all can be set with egg in this way to make various versions of fritatas and tortillas and what has ubiquitously come to be known as Spanish Omelette.

SERVES
8–10

INGREDIENTS

- 500 g / 1 lb short-grain organic brown rice
- 100 g / 4 oz wild rice
- 125 ml / 5 fl oz olive oil
- 300 g / 10 oz onions, diced
- 2–3 cloves garlic, crushed
- 1 kg / 2 lb tinned tomatoes, drained and chopped
- 1 large sprig fresh basil
- 1 sprig fresh marjoram, oregano or thyme
- 750 g / 1½ lb aubergine, cut into 1 cm / ½ in slices
- dash of Tabasco
- 125 g / 5 oz Cheddar cheese, grated
- 4 eggs, size 3, beaten
- 50 g / 2 oz rolled oats
- 1 tbsp chopped basil
- 500 g / 1 lb tomatoes, sliced and seasoned with salt, pepper, garlic and Tabasco
- salt and freshly ground black pepper

METHOD

Cook the brown rice with the wild rice until tender (see recipe for Rice and Courgette Timbales, page 23). In the meantime, heat a little less than half the olive oil and fry the onion and garlic until transparent. Add the drained and chopped tinned tomatoes as well as most of the basil and marjoram and simmer for 15–20 minutes until further reduced to make a thick sauce.

Meanwhile, baste the aubergine slices with the remaining olive oil and sprinkle with a little salt and a dash of Tabasco. Place under a hot grill until golden brown on both sides. Set aside.

Remove the wilted herbs from the tomato sauce. Mix the rice with the grated cheese, tomato sauce, beaten eggs, rolled oats and the chopped basil. Mix well and set aside.

Preheat the oven to 200°C/400°F/gas 6. Very lightly oil a cake tin or round foil container 25 cm / 10 in in diameter and line with most of the aubergine slices. Then press down about half the rice mixture so it reaches halfway up the tin. Add the remaining aubergine slices and the tomato slices. Add the rest of the rice, again making sure that it is well pressed down.

Bake for 35–40 minutes or until firm. Allow to cool for a few minutes, then run a sharp knife around the edge and turn out onto a large plate. Eat hot or cold.

RICE AND COURGETTE TIMBALES

Substantial enough to make a meal with little more than a mixed salad, these timbales are popular at Cranks. The most important thing, as in all recipes which call for the use of brown rice, is to cook the rice properly. The rice needs to be rinsed first, then covered with one and a half times its volume in water and brought to the boil. The heat is then reduced and the rice simmered for a further 45 minutes, covered with a lid, until all the water is absorbed and the rice is tender. Some, in the pursuit of health, seem to think that brown rice should be *al dente* – please let that be another wholefood misconception to bite the dust. You may add a little tamari or sea salt to the boiling water if you like.

SERVES

6

INGREDIENTS

- 150 g / 6 oz short-grain Italian, organic brown rice
- 1 tbsp sunflower oil
- 50 g / 2 oz onions, diced
- 100 g / 4 oz carrots, cut into a julienne
- 2–3 cloves garlic, crushed
- 100 g / 4 oz courgettes, cut into a julienne
- 1 tbsp sesame seeds

- 1 tbsp tahini
- 1 tsp cumin
- dash of Tabasco
- 1 tbsp parsley, finely chopped
- 1 tbsp coriander leaves, finely chopped
- salt and freshly ground black pepper

METHOD

Bring the rice to the boil as described above. Meanwhile, heat the sunflower oil and sauté the onion until transparent. Add the carrots and half the garlic and sauté for no more than 1 minute. Remove from the pan and sauté the courgettes together with the remaining garlic and sesame seeds for no more than 30 seconds. Add the tahini, cumin, Tabasco, parsley, coriander and seasoning to the cooked rice, then the carrots and finally half the courgettes. Divide the reserved courgettes between six moulds, 7.5 cm / 3 in in diameter, and press down gently with your fingers. Press the rice mixture firmly onto the courgettes and turn out. Eat warm or cold, with a mixed salad.

DEEP-FRIED WONTONS

WITH GREEN BEANS AND ASPARAGUS
IN BLACK BEAN SAUCE

Fresh wonton skins can be bought in Chinese supermarkets.
This dish also works well as a main course.

INGREDIENTS

- 1 litre / 2 pints sunflower oil
- 150 g / 6 oz leeks, finely sliced
- 1 medium carrot, shredded
- 1 medium courgette, grated or cut into a julienne
- 1 spring onion, finely sliced
- 50 g / 2 oz tofu, crumbled and soaked in 2 tbsp hot water and ½ tsp bouillon powder
- 2 cloves garlic, finely crushed
- 1 piece grated ginger, to taste
- 2.5 cm / 1 in piece chilli, finely chopped
- ½ tsp ground coriander
- dash of Tabasco
- ¼ tsp black bean sauce
- 50 g / 2 oz whole almonds, lightly toasted and chopped
- 2 tsp lime juice
- pinch of ground nutmeg
- 18 wonton skins
- salt and freshly ground black pepper

TO SERVE

- 1 tbsp sunflower oil
- ½ red pepper. diced into 5 mm / ¼ in pieces
- ½ yellow pepper, diced into 5 mm / ¼ in pieces
- Tabasco
- 500 g / 1 lb green beans, blanched in salted water for 5 minutes
- 125 g / 5 oz asparagus, 12.5 cm / 5 in long, blanched in salted water for 5 minutes
- 100 ml / 4 fl oz water, reserved from blanching the vegetables
- 2 tbsp black bean sauce

METHOD

Heat 1 tbsp of the oil in a pan and fry the sliced leeks for 1 minute until transparent. Add the shredded carrot, courgette and spring onion and the drained tofu. Add the garlic, ginger, chopped chilli and ground coriander and continue to fry for 1–2 minutes. Add a dash of Tabasco and the black bean sauce. Season with salt and pepper and remove from heat. Add the almonds, which should be quite small but not as smooth as commercial ground almonds and still include some bigger pieces, and the lime juice and nutmeg. Allow to cool slightly, then work with your fingers for a few seconds until the ingredients are well mixed together. Shape into 18 equal-sized balls and set aside.

Meanwhile, lay out the wonton squares and place a ball of mixture on the centre of each. Moisten the edges all the way round with a little water, using your fingers or a pastry brush. Bring the four corners up to meet in the middle and press the sides together so you end up with a pointed four-cornered purse.

Line a colander with at least two layers of kitchen paper. Heat the remaining oil in a pan until hot and gently drop in the filled wontons, three or four at a time. Fry for 2 minutes until golden brown all the way round. You may need to turn them around with two forks and to hold them down as they tend to fall on one side and stay that way. Remove from the oil and immediately transfer to the colander.

For the green beans, heat half the oil and quickly sauté the diced red and yellow peppers, with just a little salt and pepper and a dash of Tabasco and set aside. Heat the rest of the oil in the same pan and sauté the blanched green beans and asparagus for a minute or two. Add the black bean sauce and the reserved blanching water. Stir and sauté on a high heat for 2 minutes, adding a dash of Tabasco, until the liquid is half reduced but be sure there is enough sauce to generously coat the vegetables. Return the red and yellow peppers to the pan and sauté for a further 30 seconds. Divide the green bean mixture between 6 plates, place 3 wontons on each and serve.

SPINACH AND SUNDRIED TOMATO ROULADE

WITH A CREAM CHEESE
AND FLAKED ALMOND FILLING

This is the ideal starter to make for a dinner party as the result is very impressive, and it can easily be made in advance.

INGREDIENTS

- 12 eggs, size 3
- 300 g / 10 oz frozen spinach, thawed and squeezed of excess water
- 2 cloves garlic, crushed
- pinch of nutmeg
- 2 tbsp very red sundried tomato purée
- salt and freshly ground black pepper

FOR THE FILLING

- 1 tbsp flaked almonds, lightly toasted
- 1 tbsp chives, finely chopped
- 250 g / 8 oz low-fat cream cheese

METHOD

Prepare a baking tray 40 x 35 cm / 16 x 14 in by lining it with baking parchment, generously spread with butter. Preheat the oven to 170°C/325°F/gas 3.

Place 6 egg yolks in one bowl and 6 in another, and set the whites aside. Add the drained spinach, a little salt, pepper, crushed garlic and nutmeg to one bowl and the sundried tomato purée to the other. Whisk the egg whites in a separate bowl until they are stiff and stand in peaks and divide equally between the two bowls. Fold in gently with a metal spoon until well incorporated. Spread the spinach mixture along the whole length and half the width of the tray and then spread the tomato mixture along the other so you end up with two parallel strips. Place immediately in the preheated oven for 14 minutes, or until set. Allow to cool.

Meanwhile, make the filling by adding the flaked almonds and chives to the cream cheese. Place a piece of cling film larger than the roulade itself onto a clean work surface and turn the roulade out onto it. When it is completely cold, spread the cream cheese mixture carefully with a palette knife, leaving a 1 cm / ½ in gap around the edges as the filling will spread as you roll the roulade. Roll up gently from the bottom as you would a Swiss roll.

To serve, trim both ends so that all three colours show and slice. The roulade can be kept tightly wrapped up in cling film in the fridge for up to two days.

RAVIOLI

WITH THREE FILLINGS IN ROSEMARY, GARLIC AND LIME BUTTER

I have given this as a starter recipe, only because making sufficient pouches for a main course may seem daunting. But by doubling the recipe, you will have quite enough for a dinner party for 6. The pouches are a full 5 cm / 2 in in diameter by the time the edges have been pressed out so 3 each for a starter is sufficient.

A thin wooden rolling pin does the job of rolling best of all and you do not need to use a pasta machine. I used mine just once and it has been sitting at the back of a cupboard ever since.

SERVES

6

INGREDIENTS

FOR THE PASTA

- 350 g / 12 oz strong plain flour or Farina "00" (available from Italian delicatessens and some supermarkets)
- 3 eggs, size 2
- 2 tbsp milk

FOR THE FILLINGS

- 150 g / 6 oz ricotta
- 15 g / ½ oz matzo meal or fine breadcrumbs
- 1 ½ tsp fresh grated Parmesan cheese
- 1 clove garlic, crushed
- 50 g / 2 oz rocket, wilted in ½ tsp heated butter for 30 seconds

- 50 g / 2 oz reconstituted dried mushrooms, chopped and sautéed in ½ tsp butter
- 3–4 asparagus spears, blanched and roughly chopped into small pieces

FOR THE ROSEMARY BUTTER

- 150 g / 6 oz butter
- 1 shallot, very finely diced
- 2–3 cloves garlic
- juice and zest of ½ lime
- 1 large sprig rosemary, leaves stripped

METHOD

To make the pasta, pile the flour onto the work surface and make a well in the centre. Lightly whisk the eggs and 1 tbsp milk in a bowl and slowly pour into the well, gradually drawing in the flour with your hands until it is all absorbed. Then knead the dough for 8 minutes to form a smooth ball. Finally, divide the ball into two, wrap each half with cling film and allow to rest for 30 minutes.

To make the fillings, divide the ricotta into 3 equal amounts and add the equally divided matzo meal or breadcrumbs, the Parmesan and garlic to each lot. Then add the mushrooms to one, the rocket to the second and the asparagus to the third.

Allowing yourself plenty of space to work in, lightly flour the work surface. Roll out two pieces of pasta of equal size, side by side (you may need to start with pieces smaller than the original two balls) using a well-floured, thin wooden rolling pin.

Turn the pasta one quarter turn after each application of the rolling pin. Work in one direction only, rolling away from yourself, so that you are not so much rolling out the pasta as pushing it and stretching it away from you. Lift the pasta occasionally to make sure that it is not sticking to the surface and add a little more flour if necessary. The pasta, when rolled to the correct thickness, should be as thin as a silk scarf.

Place teaspoons of the filling at equal intervals on one sheet of pasta, using a round biscuit cutter 5 cm / 2 in in diameter to help you mark out the gaps. Do not cut all the way through the pasta at this stage. Brush a little of the remaining milk around each circle.

Lift the second piece of pasta with the rolling pin and lay carefully on top of the first. Press down around the filling, with the milk helping to seal the two sheets of pasta together. Now cut out with the pastry cutter. Lift each pouch from the work surface and, with lightly floured fingers, press the edges even closer together so that the edges are barely thicker than the single layered centres. Lay on lightly floured plastic trays or boards.

To cook the pasta pouches, bring a large pan of salted water to the boil. Drop the pouches in one at a time but working quickly. Cook for 3–4 minutes, testing that they are tender before removing them with a slotted spoon.

For the rosemary butter, melt the butter and add the finely diced shallot and crushed garlic. Whisk quickly with a fork or small hand whisk for few seconds and then add the lime juice, zest and rosemary. Stir again for a few seconds. Place 3 pouches on each plate, pour the rosemary butter over and serve.

GATEAU DE CREPES FLORENTINES

A colourful and easy recipe that is good hot or cold – perfect as a summer's lunch and equally at home on a party buffet. Almost any combination of sauces works but always have 3. The crêpes should be fine and lacy. You actually need only seven pancakes for one gâteau but the recipe is for 12 because I know it is practically impossible to resist eating 1 or 2 as you go along.

INGREDIENTS

SERVES
12

FOR THE CREPES
- 150 g / 6 oz plain flour, sifted
- 2 eggs, size 1
- 250 ml / 10 fl oz milk, skimmed or full fat
- 125 ml / 5 fl oz water
- 2 tbsp olive oil
- pinch of salt

METHOD

Mix all the ingredients except 1 tbsp of olive oil together in a blender and blend thoroughly. Leave to stand for 2 hours.

Oil the base of a crêpe pan or other shallow, cast-iron pan with a piece of kitchen paper dipped into oil (you can use a non-stick frying or pancake pan but these don't tend to have a very long shelf life). Heat until a spoonful of the mixture dropped onto the pan sizzles immediately.

Pour in one small ladleful of the batter and tip the pan all around so that the batter covers it completely. Cook until golden brown underneath, then turn or toss over and cook on the other side. Slide the crêpe onto a plate and repeat, oiling the pan in between each, until all the batter is used up.

INGREDIENTS

FOR THE AUBERGINE FILLING
- I large aubergine, cut into 5 mm / ¼ in slices
- 2 tbsp olive oil
- dash of Tabasco
- dash of balsamic vinegar
- 2 cloves garlic, crushed
- salt

FOR THE PEA-FENNEL FILLING
- 125 g / 5 oz petits pois
- 40 g / 1½ oz butter
- I bulb fennel, cut into 2.5 cm / 1 in chunks
- 2 cloves garlic, crushed
- I tsp bouillon powder mixed with 5 tbsp hot water
- 25 g / 1 oz plain unbleached flour

- 50 ml / 2 fl oz milk
- 50 ml / 2 fl oz double cream
- salt and freshly ground black pepper

FOR THE TOMATO-OLIVE FILLING
- 2–3 tbsp olive oil
- I large onion, diced
- 400 g / 14 oz tin tomatoes, drained
- 2 cloves garlic, crushed
- several leaves of basil
- 100 g / 4 oz black olives, pitted

FOR THE TOPPING
- 25 g / 1 oz freshly grated Parmesan cheese
- I tbsp finely chopped herb of your choice

METHOD

For the aubergine filling, baste the aubergine slices with olive oil and season with salt, Tabasco and balsamic vinegar. Place under a hot grill and brown on both sides for 4–5 minutes. Remove from heat and immediately add the crushed garlic, taking care not to break up the slices in the process. Set aside.

For the pea-fennel filling, place the petits pois in a pan of boiling salted water and blanch for 3–4 minutes. Remove from the heat and refresh under cold water. Melt the butter in a pan and sauté the fennel with the crushed garlic. Add the bouillon, cover with a lid and simmer gently for 4–5 minutes until the fennel is braised and soft. Add the petits pois and then sprinkle the flour over. Stir carefully until the flour is all absorbed. Add the milk and stir until the mixture thickens. Bring to the boil, stirring constantly, and finally add the cream, stirring for a couple of minutes, season and set aside.

To make the tomato filling, heat the olive oil and sauté the onion until transparent. Add the drained tomatoes, garlic and basil leaves. Reduce for about 15 minutes, stirring regularly. Add the black olives. At the last minute, remove the basil leaves.

Preheat the oven to 180°C/350°F/gas 4. Lightly oil a round ovenproof dish and place one pancake in it. Assemble, alternating pancakes with the different fillings, until they are all used up. Finish with a pancake. Cover with foil and bake for 10–15 minutes until hot. Turn out onto a large plate. Sprinkle with Parmesan and finely chopped herbs, and wait a few minutes before cutting to allow the gâteau to settle.

COUSCOUS TERRINE

WITH GRILLED RED PEPPERS AND AUBERGINES

The couscous for this terrine needs to be stickier than a normal light and fluffy couscous, hence the greater quantity of water given in this recipe. Serve with lime and coriander cream (see page 110).

SERVES

6

INGREDIENTS

- 1 tsp vegetable bouillon
- 1 litre / 2 pints boiling water
- 500 g / 1 lb couscous
- 2 medium aubergines, sliced
- 2 tbsp olive oil
- 1 large onion, diced
- 1 bunch coriander, chopped
- 1½ tsp mustard seeds

- ½ tsp grain mustard
- 2 cloves garlic, crushed
- 1 piece chilli, very finely chopped
- 3–4 tomatoes, juice and seeds removed and roughly chopped
- 2 red peppers, chargrilled, skin, pith and seeds removed, and quartered (see page 173)
- salt and freshly ground black pepper

METHOD

Dissolve the bouillon powder in the boiling water, pour over the couscous and set aside for about 10 minutes.

Preheat the grill. Baste slices of aubergine with some of the olive oil and a little salt and place under a hot grill for 5 minutes, turning halfway through the cooking time. Set aside.

Heat the remaining olive oil in a pan and fry the onion until soft. Add the fried onion to the couscous, together with the coriander, mustard seeds, grain mustard, garlic, the chopped chilli and tomatoes and further seasoning.

Line a 25 cm / 10 in loaf tin with cling film so it hangs over the edges. Line the base with slices of grilled aubergine. Then press half the couscous firmly on top and add another layer of aubergine and the quartered grilled red peppers. Press the remaining couscous on top. Bring round the overhanging cling film and refrigerate for 30 minutes.

Turn out onto a large plate. Use a finely serrated knife to cut slices no thicker than 2.5 cm / 1 in and serve with a choice of salads.

AUBERGINE CHARLOTTE

This makes a highly effective dish for a buffet table, but its stunning appearance belies its extraordinary ease of preparation. Simply ensure that the aubergine slices are well browned and the tomato sauce well reduced and garnish with fresh coriander leaves.

INGREDIENTS

- thick tomato sauce (see page 100)
- 1 tbsp sundried tomato purée
- 2 large aubergines
- 50 ml / 2 fl oz olive oil
- 50 ml / 2 fl oz Greek yoghurt
- 50 ml / 2 fl oz sour cream
- 3 cloves garlic, crushed
- pinch of nutmeg

- 1 large handful coriander, roughly chopped, plus 1 large handful for garnish
- 1 large handful parsley
- mixture of salad leaves such as sorrel, rocket, young cos, oak leaf and coriander
- 50 ml / 2 fl oz walnut oil
- salt and freshly ground black pepper

METHOD

Preheat the oven to 180°C/350°F/gas 4. Mix the tomato sauce and sundried tomato purée and set aside.

Slice the aubergines into 1 cm / ½ in slices, baste with olive oil and bake in the oven for about 20 minutes, turning over halfway through the cooking time, until golden brown on both sides. Alternatively, place the basted slices under a hot grill for 5 minutes, turning them over so that both sides brown.

Mix the yoghurt, sour cream, garlic, nutmeg, fresh herbs and salt and pepper.

Line the base of a round ovenproof dish with the aubergine slices. Then top with the tomato sauce, another layer of aubergine, then the yoghurt and cream mixture, and end with aubergine slices. Bake in the preheated oven for 30–35 minutes then set aside to cool.

Toss the salad leaves with the oil and seasoning. Run a knife around the sides of the charlotte and turn out onto a large round plate, abundantly garnished with the salad leaves. Separate the remaining coriander leaves from their stalks and press onto the charlotte's surface. Serve with chunks of ciabatta, riddled with sundried tomato.

SPINACH RISOTTO PIE

If you are a risotto fan as I am but cannot quite handle it
as a summer meal, then try this baked risotto which is just
as delicious eaten cold.

SERVES
8 – 1 0

INGREDIENTS

- 25 g / 1 oz bouillon powder
- 1 litre / 2 pints boiling water
- 50 ml / 2 fl oz olive oil
- 250 g / 8 oz onions, diced
- 3 cloves garlic, crushed
- pinch of nutmeg

- 500 g / 1 lb Arborio rice
- 500g / 1 lb fresh spinach
- 100 g / 4 oz Parmesan cheese, grated
- 6 eggs, size 3, beaten
- 1–2 tomatoes, cut into slices
- salt and freshly ground black pepper

METHOD

Preheat the oven to 200°C/400°F/gas 6.

Make a stock with the bouillon powder and boiling water and keep warm. Heat the
oil and add the onion, garlic and nutmeg. Fry until transparent. Now add the rice and
also fry until transparent, stirring all the time. Add the stock gradually, stirring
continuously, until it is all absorbed and the grains are creamy but still intact. Add the
spinach and stir until it is wilted. Finally add the Parmesan and then the beaten eggs.

Oil a round ovenproof dish and line with the tomato slices and season. Add the rice
mixture and bake in the preheated oven for 20–25 minutes. Run a knife around the pie
and turn out. Eat hot or cold.

FETA CHEESE AND SUNDRIED TOMATO SOUFFLE

SPIKED WITH FRESH HERBS AND BLACK OLIVES

You get a lot of mileage out of an egg as you'll see from this recipe, which puffs and puffs, yet at the same time stays rich and creamy with a wonderful melting texture. Since a soufflé is little more than white sauce (and everyone knows how to make white sauce!) with added yolks and whisked egg whites, there is no reason for fear. It may all look like magic – all that whisking of egg whites creating millions of air bubbles which expand during baking. A few tricks help. Add a drop of lemon juice to the egg whites to prevent them from splitting and separating and follow the old adage of using a spotlessly clean and dry bowl when whisking the egg whites. Be scrupulous about this. Also, do not remove the soufflé from the oven as soon as it has risen but let it sit there for a few seconds first.

SERVES

6

INGREDIENTS

- 75 g / 3 oz unsalted butter
- 75 g / 3 oz plain flour
- 350 ml / 12 fl oz milk
- 150 g / 6 oz young, moist Feta cheese, crumbled
- 2 tbsp sundried tomato purée
- 1–2 basil leaves, finely shredded
- 2 cloves garlic, preferably cooked first and mashed to a purée
- 5 large egg yolks
- 9 large egg whites
- juice of half a small lemon
- salt and freshly ground black pepper

TO LINE THE SOUFFLE DISH:

- 1 heaped tbsp unsalted butter, softened
- 25 g / 1 oz fresh Parmesan cheese, finely grated

METHOD

Preheat the oven to 190°C/375°F/gas 5 and place a baking sheet in it. Generously butter the sides of a 1.5 litre / 3 pint soufflé dish and add the Parmesan. Shake it all around so that it sticks to the butter and discard any excess. Chill until needed.

To make the white sauce, bring the milk to the boil. Melt the butter in a saucepan without letting it brown. Add the flour and stir for 1 minute. Gradually add the hot milk to the butter and flour mixture, stirring all the time until you have a smooth white sauce.

Remove from the heat and cool for a few minutes, again stirring, this time to prevent a skin from forming. Add the crumbled Feta cheese, basil, sundried tomato purée, garlic and the egg yolks. Whisk with a hand-held whisk for a few moments. Season with a little salt and pepper.

In another bowl, whisk the egg whites to very soft peaks, then add the lemon juice. Continue whisking to firm peaks. Whisk a quarter of these into the cheese sauce base, then fold in the rest using a rubber spatula. Use the spatula again to scoop the soufflé mixture carefully into the soufflé dish, then run it along the inside of the dish to create a slight gap between the mixture and the dish. Bake in the preheated oven for 20–25 minutes until well risen and golden. Serve and eat immediately.

soups

Nothing is more evocative of home cooking than a good soup. Recipes range from the prosaic mixed vegetable to the sophisticated wild garlic and blood orange, yet neither requires any great skill or complex technique.

When making soup, good ingredients are essential, and good stock is absolutely vital. Though it is possible to use ready-made stock, nothing quite parallels the subtleties of a home-made stock. For a light stock, use light coloured vegetables such as celery (leaves and all), leeks, onions, carrots, garlic, a handful of fresh parsley. For a dark stock add to these a handful of brown lentils, some field mushrooms, a little tamari, bay leaves and other herbs of your choice. Cover completely with water and bring to the boil, then simmer gently for at least 1 hour, until all the vegetables are soft and every bit of flavour has been extracted from them. Though soups are often served as a first course many soups can be described as 'a meal in a bowl'. Additions of cheese, croûtons, fresh herbs and lightly sautéed diced vegetables all contribute to a nourishing and satisfying meal.

CURRIED PARSNIP SOUP

I suppose that this is the kind of combination for which the term Anglo-Indian is a perfect fit. If possible, use small parsnips with no trace of woodiness.

SERVES

6

INGREDIENTS

- 25 ml / 1 fl oz sunflower oil
- 1 onion, peeled and diced
- 1 potato, peeled and diced
- 1 tbsp mild garam masala
- 1 tsp ground coriander
- seeds from 2 cardamom pods, crushed

- 1 kg / 2 lb parsnips, peeled, trimmed and chopped into 1 cm / ½ in pieces.
- 2–2.5 litres / 4–5 pints vegetable stock or water
- 1 garlic clove, left whole
- 200 ml / 8 fl oz double cream
- salt and freshly ground black pepper

METHOD

Heat the oil in a large saucepan and fry the onion until transparent. Halfway through, add the diced potato and fry until this is also transparent. Add the garam masala, coriander and crushed cardamom seeds. Stir for 2–3 minutes, adding a little water to loosen the spices. Add the chopped parsnips and sauté for 3–4 minutes. Add half the water or stock and the garlic clove and bring to the boil. Reduce the heat and simmer gently for about 15 minutes until the parsnips are tender when poked with a fork, then blend in an electric blender until absolutely smooth and return to the pan. Add the rest of the water and bring back to the boil. Stir in the double cream and heat to boiling point. Adjust the seasoning if necessary and serve.

CARROT SOUP

WITH LIME, CORIANDER, COCONUT AND SPINACH

Bulky vegetables such as carrot can be turned into the creamiest soups with barely any additional cream as long as you use a good blender. I've added ground almonds or you could use very finely ground cashew nuts, loosened with a little water to make a cashew butter. Both make the soup rich and nutritious. I always make this kind of soup in a pressure cooker, only adding the nuts and seasoning at the end.

SERVES

6

INGREDIENTS

- 1 kg / 2 lb carrots, peeled and cut into 2.5 cm / 1 in slices
- 1 large onion, cut into quarters
- 1 tbsp bouillon powder
- 1 clove garlic, left whole
- 50 g / 2 oz ground almonds
- 25 g / 1 oz creamed coconut
- juice of 1 lime
- 250 g / 8 oz fresh spinach
- Greek yoghurt or crème fraîche
- fresh coriander leaves
- chunk of fresh coconut, finely shaved (optional)
- salt and freshly ground black pepper

METHOD

Place the carrots in a pressure cooker with the onion, bouillon powder, whole garlic clove, a little salt and enough water to cover. Bring to the boil and then cook under gentle pressure for 10 minutes or until the carrots are tender. Remove the garlic clove and pour the soup into a blender with the ground almonds. Blend until absolutely smooth.

Return to the heat and add the creamed coconut until it is dissolved, then the lime juice and finally the spinach. Add a little water if the consistency looks too thick. Stir long enough for the spinach to wilt and remove from heat.

Serve at once with a dollop of Greek yoghurt or crème fraîche, black pepper, coriander leaves and a few shavings of fresh coconut.

OLD-FASHIONED LENTIL SOUP

This soup is delicious when first made but even better the next day when the flavours have had time to develop. You could add a handful of fresh spinach at the end or a red pepper, chargrilled, peeled and cut into thin strips (see page 173).

(see page 173).

SERVES
6

INGREDIENTS

- 75 ml / 3 fl oz olive oil
- I large onion, peeled and diced
- 5 ml / I tsp cumin
- 3 medium carrots, peeled and chopped
- I medium potato, peeled and diced
- 500 g / I lb brown lentils
- 3–4 cloves garlic, peeled and left whole

- 2.5 litres / 4½ pints vegetable stock or water
- 15–30 ml / 1–2 tbsp tamari
- dash of Tabasco
- small bunch parsley, finely chopped
- 1–2 spring onions, finely sliced
- salt and freshly ground black pepper

METHOD

Heat 1 tbsp oil in a large heavy based saucepan and sauté the onion with the cumin until transparent. Then add the carrots and potato and sauté for a couple of minutes. Add the lentils, whole garlic cloves and half the water. Bring to the boil, then reduce the heat and simmer for 20 minutes or so, stirring occasionally to prevent the soup from sticking to the bottom. Add the rest of the water and continue to cook slowly for a further 20 – 25 minutes until the lentils are tender and the soup quite substantial in appearance. Add the remaining olive oil, the tamari, Tabasco and seasoning. Just before serving, stir in the fresh parsley and spring onions.

RED ONION SOUP

WITH TOASTED CHEESE FLOATS

I am a great fan of red onions and thought I was being original when I made this soup. Then I looked through Louise Pickford's beautiful book, *The Inspired Vegetarian*, and there of course it was – lodged in my memory from an earlier perusal no doubt, though our seasoning differs and I have retained the Gruyère of the original French recipe instead of Louise's goat's cheese for the toasts.

SERVES

6

INGREDIENTS

- 125 ml / 5 fl oz olive oil
- 1.5 kg / 3 lb red onions, peeled and thinly sliced
- 3–4 cloves garlic, crushed
- 5 ml /1 tsp basil, chopped
- 5 ml / 1 tsp marjoram, chopped
- 1 bay leaf
- 150 ml / 6 fl oz marsala or port wine

- 1 litre / 2 pints dark vegetable stock (see page 42)
- 15–30 ml / 1–2 tbsp tamari
- salt and freshly ground black pepper

FOR THE CHEESE TOASTS

- 6 pieces of French bread, cut into 1 cm / ½ in slices
- 75 g / 3 oz Gruyère cheese, grated

METHOD

Heat the oil in a pan and sauté the onions over a medium heat for 25–30 minutes, stirring regularly to prevent the onions from sticking and burning. Add the garlic and the herbs, then most of the wine or port. Simmer and reduce the liquid to about half. Then add the stock and bring to the boil, then lower the heat and simmer gently for a further 20 minutes. Add the remaining wine and the tamari and simmer for another couple of minutes. Taste for seasoning.

Just before serving, prepare the toasts, lay the bread under a grill and toast lightly on both sides. Pile some of the grated Gruyère onto one side. Pour the soup into heatproof bowls and place a toast in each bowl. Return the bowls to the grill until the cheese is melted and golden brown and serve at once.

CARIBBEAN PEPPERPOT

This is a very popular item on the Cranks menu. Garnished with the peppers, the soup is vibrant, fragrant and colourful.

SERVES

6

INGREDIENTS

- 5 tbsp sunflower oil
- 150 g / 6 oz onions, diced
- 3 cloves garlic, finely chopped
- 300 g / 10 oz potatoes, cut into 5 mm / ¼ in dice
- ½ tsp bouillon powder, dissolved in 250 ml / 10 fl oz hot water
- 100 g / 4 oz white cabbage, diced
- 400 g / 14 oz tin chopped tomatoes
- 1 heaped tbsp paprika
- 1 heaped tsp ground coriander
- dash of Tabasco

- ½ tsp ground chilli powder
- 1 piece fresh chilli, finely chopped
- 400 ml / 14 fl oz coconut milk
- pinch of soft brown sugar (optional)

FOR THE PEPPERS

- 1 tbsp sunflower oil
- 1 red pepper, cut into 5 mm / ¼ in dice
- 1 yellow pepper, cut into 5 mm / ¼ in dice
- dash of Tabasco
- 1–2 tbsp tamari

METHOD

Heat the oil and sauté the diced onion and garlic until transparent. Add the diced potatoes until they too are transparent. Add 4 tbsp of the hot bouillon, stir and cook for 1 minute or so. Then add the diced cabbage and sauté for 2–3 minutes. Drain the chopped tomatoes, reserving the juice. Add the tomatoes to the soup together with the paprika, ground coriander, Tabasco and chilli powder. Stir well and add a further 150 ml / 6 fl oz of the hot bouillon, the reserved tomato juice and the fresh chilli. Simmer gently for 7–8 minutes and add the coconut milk. Check the sweetness of the soup and, if necessary, add a pinch of soft brown sugar.

For the peppers, heat the oil in a frying pan and sauté the diced peppers for just a minute, until they begin to blacken in places. Add a drop or two of Tabasco and tamari to taste and set aside.

To serve, mix half the peppers into the soup and reserve the rest to use as garnish on each serving or in the soup tureen.

WILD MUSHROOM SOUP
WITH PORT

This recipe makes a small number of wild and dried mushrooms go a long way. It is a very rich soup and very elegant, the perfect starter for an Autumn dinner party.

SERVES
6 ·

INGREDIENTS

- 25 g / 1 oz dried mushrooms
- 175 ml / 7 fl oz hot water, for soaking dried mushrooms
- 50 g / 2 oz butter
- 150 g / 6 oz onions, peeled and diced
- 4 cloves garlic, crushed
- 25 g / 1 oz shiitake mushrooms, sliced

- 75 g / 3 oz mixed wild mushrooms, gently brushed or wiped clean, then trimmed
- 100 ml / 4 fl oz port
- 1 litre / 2 pints vegetable stock
- 250 ml / 10 fl oz double cream
- ½ tsp grain mustard
- salt and freshly ground black pepper

METHOD

Soak the dried mushrooms in hot water for 30 minutes until reconstituted and set aside. Drain the mushrooms, retaining the soaking liquid. Line a sieve with muslin and pour through the soaking liquid to remove any grit and set the liquid aside.

Place the butter in a saucepan and melt over a gentle heat. Add the diced onion and sauté with the garlic until brown. Add the sliced shiitake mushrooms and sauté for a further 5–6 minutes. Now add wild mushrooms and sauté again, stirring regularly, for another 3–4 minutes. Then add the dried mushrooms and the strained soaking liquid, half the port and some of the stock and cook until reduced by about half. Then blend the soup in an electric blender until smooth and return to the pan.

Add the double cream and bring gently to the boil. Add the remaining port and continue to simmer for a couple of minutes. Finally pour in the remaining stock, add the mustard, adjust the seasoning, stir well and serve.

MINESTRONE

This is a text book classic which has been adulterated in often far from flattering ways. The Cranks version is delicious, especially when served with Parmesan and better still the next day when the flavours have had time to develop.

SERVES

6

INGREDIENTS

- 3 tbsp olive oil
- I onion, peeled and diced
- 6 ripe tomatoes, peeled and chopped
- 4 medium potatoes, peeled and diced
- I litre / 2 pints vegetable stock
- 150 g / 6 oz shelled broad beans, fresh or frozen
- 100 g / 4 oz petit pois, fresh or frozen
- 75 g / 3 oz mushrooms, roughly chopped

- 150 g / 6 oz green beans, cut into small pieces
- 250 g / 8 oz courgettes, diced
- I small cauliflower, broken into small florets
- 400 g / 14 oz tin cannellini beans, drained
- 3 tbsp parsley, finely chopped
- 100 g / 4 oz small pasta shapes
- salt and freshly ground black pepper
- 75 g / 3 oz Parmesan cheese, grated

METHOD

Heat the oil in a pan and fry the onion until transparent. Add the tomatoes, salt and pepper and fry for a further 5 minutes. Now add the potatoes and half the stock. Bring to the boil and simmer until the potatoes are tender. Then add the broad beans, peas, mushrooms, green beans, courgettes, cauliflower and the remaining stock and simmer for about 25 minutes until the vegetables are very tender. Next, add the cannellini beans and heat through. Add the parsley and stir for 3–4 minutes. Bring to the boil, add the pasta and boil for 10 minutes. Serve with the freshly grated Parmesan.

BORSCHT
WITH ACCESSORIES

I have been served Borscht both by Russians and Poles who thought their version definitive. The Russian recipe, on which this is based, is thick, rich and filling. I recall that it was served with vodka, icy cold and wild, which gave a mood of extreme jollity and made the experience more authentic.

INGREDIENTS

- 1 kg / 2 lb small fresh beetroot
- 50 ml / 2 fl oz sunflower oil
- 1 large onion, peeled and diced
- 500 g / 1 lb potatoes, peeled and diced
- 75 g / 3 oz carrots, chopped
- dash of Tabasco
- 3 cloves garlic, finely chopped
- 100 ml / 4 fl oz vodka
- juice of 1 small lemon or lime
- salt and freshly ground black pepper

TO GARNISH

- 350 g / 12 oz potatoes, part-boiled and diced
- 1 litre / 2 pints sunflower oil, for deep-frying
- 150 ml / 6 fl oz Greek yoghurt or sour cream
- 1 tbsp parsley, finely chopped
- 1 tbsp dill, finely chopped

METHOD

Wash and trim the beetroot and bring to the boil in a pan of salted water. Cook for about 45 minutes until tender but still firm. Remove from the cooking liquid and reserve this for later use. Slip off the skins and chop into quarters.

Heat the oil and fry the onion until transparent and then add the diced potatoes, carrots, salt, pepper, Tabasco and chopped garlic and continue to sauté for about 5 minutes. Add the beetroot and cook for a further 2 minutes. Pour in the reserved beetroot liquid and continue to simmer gently for about 10 minutes. Add the vodka and lemon or lime juice and remove from heat. Blend until smooth with a hand-held whisk and set aside.

For the garnish, be sure the potatoes are dry (drain on kitchen paper if necessary) and deep-fry in the heated sunflower oil. (Alternatively, boil the potatoes completely and dice and omit the deep-frying.)

Serve the soup warm with a dollop of sour cream or Greek yoghurt and some finely chopped herbs on each serving, with the potatoes on the side.

CREAM OF ONION SOUP

This delicious version of French onion soup comes from
Bordeaux but I have omitted the flour and obtained the same
rich creamy texture simply by blending.

SERVES
6

INGREDIENTS

- 50 g / 2 oz butter
- 750 g / 1½ lb onions. diced
- 2–3 cloves garlic, crushed
- pinch of nutmeg
- 750 ml / 1½ pints light vegetable stock (see page 42)
- 2 egg yolks
- 100 ml / 4 fl oz double cream
- 1 tsp lemon juice
- 1 tbsp chives, snipped
- salt and freshly ground black pepper

METHOD

Heat the butter in a large heavy-based saucepan and fry the onion and garlic together
with salt, pepper and nutmeg until soft and transparent. Add the stock and stir until it
comes to the boil. Cover with a lid and simmer for 30 minutes, checking regularly that
it is not sticking to the bottom. Allow to cool for a few minutes and blend until smooth.

In a bowl, beat the egg yolks and cream with the lemon juice and gradually add in a
ladle of the hot soup. Slowly stir the egg yolk mixture back into the soup and heat
through again, but do not allow it to boil. Garnish with snipped chives and serve.

COUNTRY VEGETABLE SOUP

Some people prefer chunky soups, where they can see what they are eating, others prefer velvety smooth ones, such as this. Made in the pressure cooker and puréed in a blender, this soup – for all its ingredients – can be ready in 25 minutes.

The combination of vegetables is open to interpretation and you can be more adventurous with the seasoning or finish off with double cream, but this recipe shows how good even a very simple soup can be.

SERVES

6

INGREDIENTS

- 4–5 medium carrots, peeled and chopped
- I large onion, peeled and cut in quarters
- I bulb fennel, trimmed and cut in quarters
- 100 g / 4 oz mushrooms, oyster or open cap
- 3 leeks, trimmed and chopped
- I medium courgette, chopped
- 3 medium potatoes, peeled and chopped

- ½ small cauliflower, separated into florets
- 2 litres / 4 pints water
- I tbsp bouillon powder
- bunch of basil
- I whole head garlic, peeled
- 50 ml / 2 fl oz olive oil, or 25 g / I oz butter
- salt and freshly ground black pepper

METHOD

Place all the chopped ingredients, the water, bouillon powder, basil, garlic cloves and seasoning in a pressure cooker and bring to pressure for 10 minutes. Reduce the heat and cook under pressure for a further 10 minutes. Allow to cool slightly and blend until smooth. Stir in the olive oil or butter, adjust the seasoning if necessary and serve.

FRESH GARLIC AND BLOOD ORANGE VICHYSSOISE

WITH GARLIC LEAF AND CORIANDER

This is one of the most delicate and elegant soups going. Choose blood oranges with dark and shrivelled skins for a truly blood red juice, the effectiveness of which is simply surprising. The garlic itself is white with hints of pale green and comes apart in delicate folds of fine skin. Garlic leaf can be found in Oriental shops.

SERVES

6

INGREDIENTS

- 9 heads young fresh garlic, trimmed and tough outer leaves removed
- 40 g / 1½ oz unsalted butter
- 250 g / 8 oz new potatoes, peeled and diced into 5 mm / ¼ in cubes
- 1–1.25 litres / 2–2½ pints water

- 5–6 strands saffron
- juice from 4 blood oranges
- pinch of soft brown sugar (optional)
- handful fresh coriander, roughly chopped
- 1 fresh garlic leaf, finely shredded
- salt and freshly ground black pepper

METHOD

Slice the prepared garlic very finely, as you would an onion or leek. Melt the butter in a heavy-based saucepan and add the garlic. Simmer over a gentle heat until transparent and add the diced potatoes. Continue to cook until these too are transparent. Add some of the water and the strands of saffron and continue to simmer gently for about 15 minutes, adding the rest of the water a little at a time as needed.

Blend in an electric blender until absolutely smooth and pass through a sieve if necessary. Return to a low heat and add the orange juice and sugar and salt to taste. Garnish with the roughly chopped fresh coriander, finely shredded garlic leaf and a little freshly ground black pepper. Serve at once. This soup can also be eaten cold.

CHICKPEA SOUP
WITH LIME-INFUSED CREAM

This is a rich, intense spicy soup reminiscent of the Moroccan Harira, to which the lime cream is a welcome cooling agent. This and other pulse-based soups are best made in a pressure cooker if time is a concern. Otherwise, cook the soup slowly over a period of 1½ hours, adding a little liquid each time you see it beginning to over-thicken.

INGREDIENTS

- 5 tbsp olive oil
- I large onion, peeled and diced
- 3 cloves garlic, finely chopped
- I tbsp cumin
- 1.5–2 litres / 3–4 pints water
- I tbsp paprika
- 500 g / I lb dried chickpeas, soaked overnight
- 3 cloves garlic, left whole

- I bunch fresh coriander, roughly chopped
- dash of Tabasco
- salt and freshly ground black pepper

FOR THE LIME CREAM

- zest and juice of I lime
- 500 ml / I pint Greek yoghurt
- smattering of freshly ground nutmeg

METHOD

Heat 25 ml / 1 fl oz of the olive oil in a pressure cooker pan. Then add the onion and chopped garlic and fry until transparent. Add the cumin and fry for a minute, stirring all the time and adding 2–3 tbsp of water as soon as the mix dries out. Continue in this way, adding the paprika and about 150 ml / 6 fl oz of water.

Add the chickpeas, stirring until they are well coated in the spices. Finally add the rest of the water – about 1.5 litres / 3 pints – and the whole garlic cloves. Bring to pressure, then reduce the heat to a slow simmer for 25 minutes. Test to see that the chickpeas are completely soft and about to fall apart. Add a little water if necessary and continue to simmer uncovered for 8–10 minutes, adding the remaining olive oil at the same time. Also add salt at this stage.

To make the lime-infused cream, mix the lime zest and juice with the yoghurt and allow to sit for 20–30 minutes. Stir in some fresh ground nutmeg.

Just before serving, add the coriander, Tabasco and pepper and continue to simmer for just a couple more minutes. You can mash the soup with a potato masher so that some of it is smooth and some rough or you can blend it smooth, in which case you should wait until afterwards to add the coriander. Serve with the lime cream.

CREAM OF BROCCOLI SOUP

WITH WALNUT AND DOLCELATTE GNOCCHI

We often make a broccoli and blue cheese soup at Cranks and this is a more sophisticated way of presenting and serving it. The soup itself, if you make it in a pressure cooker, takes only 10 minutes so it's worth making these mock gnocchi to add to it. Whatever you do, don't overcook the broccoli – it needs to be tender enough to blend easily but don't cook out the bright forest green colour.

SERVES
6

INGREDIENTS

- 500 g / 1 lb broccoli, cut into small florets
- 75 g / 3 oz onions, peeled and diced
- 100 g / 4 oz potatoes, peeled and diced
- 1.25 litres / 2½ pints water
- 2 tsp bouillon powder
- 2 cloves garlic
- 4 tbsp double cream
- salt and freshly ground black pepper

FOR THE GNOCCHI

- 12 walnuts, shelled and crushed finely
- 75 g / 3 oz Dolcelatte cheese
- 100 g / 4 oz Ricotta
- 100 g / 4 oz fresh breadcrumbs
- 1 egg, size 3, beaten
- 2 tbsp toasted breadcrumbs
- 1 litre / 2 pints sunflower oil
- salt and freshly ground black pepper

METHOD

Place all the soup ingredients except the cream in a pressure cooker. Bring to the boil and simmer for 10 minutes. Blend until very smooth, then add the double cream. Adjust the seasoning and set aside.

For the gnocchi, mix walnuts into the cheeses, either with a fork or your hand, so it looks like a paste. Add all the fresh breadcrumbs.

Place the beaten egg in one shallow dish and the toasted breadcrumbs in another. Shape the cheese mixture into small walnut sized pieces and dip in the beaten egg, then in the toasted breadcrumbs. Line a colander with several layers of kitchen paper. Heat the oil until it is very hot and deep-fry the gnocchi for a minute until they are golden and crisp on the outside. Remove to the colander and serve immediately with the soup.

main courses

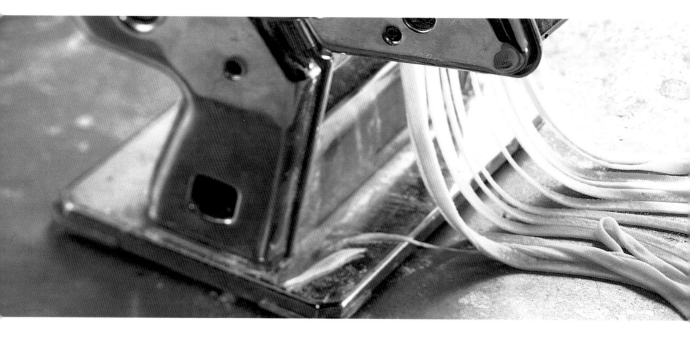

You won't find nut roasts and lentil stews in this chapter. Instead, experiment with mushroom fricassee with individual soufflés or pumpkin with noodles and coconut cream or vegetable brochettes with spiced rice.

I have never understood why main courses are thought to be the hardest part of a vegetarian meal. Perhaps the concept of meat and two veg is too hard to dispel. Yet many of the world's cuisines revolve around a selection of small dishes, with a mingling of flavours all complementing one another.

More formal occasions lend themselves to a meal with an identifiable centrepiece. It adds a sense of ceremony when there is something to cut into and to share. More informal meals are wonderful ways for everyone to sample a little bit of this and a little bit of that, each playing on a different colour or taste experience.

Then, of course, there is pasta which can be imaginative and delicious, whether served with charred vegetables, precious ingredients or simple sauces – as basic or as sophisticated as you choose.

POTATOES WITH RED ONION AND TOMATOES

This is a slowly cooked potato dish that becomes melting and soft as the thin potato slices absorb the olive oil. For a robust and warming meal, serve with a substantial salad or side vegetable dish, or serve with Filled Aubergine Rolls (see page 82).

(see page 82).

SERVES
6

INGREDIENTS

- 2 kg / 4½ lb small potatoes
- 100 ml / 4 fl oz olive oil
- I clove garlic, crushed
- I red onion, cut into thin wedges
- 8 tomatoes, cut into quarters
- salt and freshly ground black pepper
- fresh basil leaves, to garnish

METHOD

Preheat the oven to 170°C/325°F/gas 3.

Fill a large bowl with cold water. Peel the potatoes and instantly immerse them in the water to stop them going black. Cut into 2.5 mm / ⅛ in thick slices and pat the potato slices dry between two clean tea towels.

Mix them thoroughly with the olive oil, salt, pepper and crushed garlic, then pack closely into an ovenproof dish. Arrange the red onion and tomato slices, poking them down a bit on the top so that they are only partly exposed – they will burn if they are overexposed. Cover the dish with a lid or a piece of baking parchment (not foil as this can react with the tomatoes and turn the whole dish black).

Bake in the preheated oven for 45–50 minutes. Remove the lid and turn the heat up to 200°C/400°F/gas 6 and bake for a further 10 minutes until the top layer is gently crisped. Serve hot, garnished with the basil.

TAGLIATELLE

WITH BROAD BEANS, SAFFRON AND SUNDRIED VEGETABLES

Sundried aubergines, peppers and courgettes can be found in specialist Italian delicatessens. In their absence, slice half an aubergine into slices 2.5 mm / ⅛ in thick and a courgette into slices just slightly thicker than that. Brush very lightly with olive oil and sprinkle with sea salt. Place in an oven set at its lowest heat and bake, or more accurately dry out, for 1–2 hours. Cut into thin strips and proceed.

SERVES
6 – 8

INGREDIENTS

- 750 g / 1½ lb broad beans, fresh or frozen
- 750 g / 1½ lb green tagliatelle
- 125 ml / 5 fl oz olive oil
- 3 cloves garlic, finely sliced
- 150 g / 6 oz sundried vegetables – mixture of courgettes and aubergines, and tomatoes in oil, all cut into thin strips

- 5–6 strands saffron, soaked in 50 ml / 2 fl oz boiling water
- 50–200 ml / 2–8 fl oz double cream
- several basil leaves
- 75 g / 3 oz Parmesan cheese, freshly grated
- salt and freshly ground black pepper

METHOD

Blanch both fresh and frozen broad beans in salted water for 2 minutes, refresh quickly under cold water and split the skins to slide out the bright green beans. Set aside.

Cook the tagliatelle in plenty of salted water with the addition of 1 tbsp of the olive oil which helps the pasta not to stick together. Turn the pasta once or twice with a fork to separate it and when the water has returned to the boil, lower the heat so it does not boil over. When *al dente*, transfer to a large sieve or fine colander and run under cold water for a few seconds, separating the strands of pasta if necessary.

Heat the remaining olive oil over a gentle heat and add first the sliced garlic and 30 seconds later, the sundried vegetables. Add the saffron stock. Simmer for 5 minutes or so and add the tagliatelle and cream to taste. Bring to a gentle bubble and immediately add the shelled, blanched broad beans, stirring very gently for just as long as it takes to heat them through too.

Pour the tagliatelle and vegetables onto a large warmed pasta plate or bowl and add the basil and Parmesan. Toss and serve immediately.

PASTA WITH ARTICHOKE HEARTS, PINE NUTS AND GREEN OLIVES

I use supermarket spiralli pasta but the choice of pasta is pretty much up to you, although a heartier, fuller shape is preferable to a thinner, more delicate one.

SERVES

6

INGREDIENTS

- 6 small artichokes
- 150 ml / 6 fl oz olive oil
- dash of Tabasco
- 2 cloves garlic, crushed
- 1 tbsp balsamic vinegar
- 500 g / 1 lb spiralli pasta

- 250 g / 8 oz lemon-stuffed green olives, sliced or left whole
- 100 g / 4 oz pine nuts, lightly toasted
- handful of coriander leaves, roughly chopped
- 75 g / 3 oz grated Parmesan cheese (optional)
- salt and freshly ground black pepper

METHOD

Prepare the artichokes by removing the outer leaves to reveal the purple and white ones and trimming these to 3 cm / 1¼ in in length. Peel the stem of all its fibrous and inedible outer layer and then cut the artichokes in half across the length. Take out the choke and cut in half again so you end up with each artichoke cut into quarters. Baste with some of the olive oil, salt, pepper and Tabasco, then place under a hot grill for about 20 minutes, turning over at least once in the process. Remove from heat and marinate in the remaining olive oil (reserving 1 tbsp), crushed garlic and balsamic vinegar, for at least 1 hour.

Bring a large pan of salted water to the boil, add the reserved spoon of olive oil. Add the pasta, stirring once at the beginning to loosen it and prevent it sticking together. Lower the heat and follow packet instructions regarding timing.

Drain and refresh briefly under cold water. Quickly return to the pan and add the artichoke hearts and the marinade, as well as the green olives. Heat through quickly, tossing the ingredients about and finish off at the last moment with the pine nuts, coriander, and seasoning to taste. Serve at once with the grated Parmesan if desired.

PENNE WITH SUNDRIED TOMATO AND CREAM SAUCE

Sundried tomatoes are no longer a rarity. Their strong and distinctive flavour means that just a small amount cut into slivers can immediately elevate a dish from ordinary to sublime. Even more delicious is sundried tomato purée, which can be added to dressings and sauces, or spread on Bruschetta or even plain ordinary toast, or whisked into ricotta to make a light mousse.

Some ready-made sundried tomato purée is bright red and slightly sweetened, which is no bad thing. If you make your own, adding a touch of caster sugar just rounds off the taste. Simply blend the contents of a jar, including the oil they are preserved in, until very smooth.

SERVES
6

INGREDIENTS

- thick tomato sauce (see page 100)
- 500 g / 1 lb penne
- 1 tbsp olive oil
- handful of basil
- 50 g / 2 oz sundried tomatoes in oil, cut into thin slivers
- 250 g / 8 oz sundried tomato purée
- 250 ml / 8 fl oz double cream
- salt and freshly ground black pepper

METHOD

Add the pasta to a pan of boiling salted water with the olive oil and cook according to package instructions until *al dente*. Remove from the heat, drain and refresh. Meanwhile, heat the tomato sauce in a large pan. Add half the basil, the sundried tomato slivers and the sundried tomato purée. Briefly bring to the boil and add the double cream. Stir and bring to boiling point. Add the pasta and mix well. Serve immediately, garnished with the remaining basil and black pepper.

RICE AND VEGETABLE BIRYANI

I cannot vouch for the absolute authenticity of this dish. For a start, I use butter and olive oil instead of the more traditional ghee. It is just reminiscent of the kind of dish I ate in Kashmir many years ago. After eight months of living in India, the milder, sweeter, creamier dishes were manna. Rice and vegetable biryani makes a frequent and well received appearance on the Cranks menu.

SERVES
4 – 6

INGREDIENTS

FOR THE VEGETABLE CURRY

- 25 g / 1 oz butter
- 200 ml / 8 fl oz olive oil
- 300 g / 10 oz onions, diced
- 4 cardamom pods, seeds scooped out and pounded in a pestle and mortar
- 1 tbsp cumin
- 1 heaped tsp ground coriander
- 1 heaped tsp ground ginger
- ¼ tsp mustard seeds
- 3–4 cloves
- ¼ tsp dried fiery red chillis, finely chopped
- 4 cloves garlic, crushed
- 750 ml / 1½ pints water
- 250 g / 8 oz potatoes, diced
- 250 g / 8 oz carrots, peeled and cut into slices, 1 cm / ½ in thick
- 3 medium tomatoes, quartered
- 500 g / 1 lb cauliflower, trimmed and separated into small florets
- large pinch of saffron
- 250 g / 8 oz small courgettes, cut into 1 cm / ½ in slices

- 50 g / 2 oz coconut butter
- few drops of tamarind juice (optional)
- 1 bunch fresh coriander, roughly chopped
- salt

FOR THE RICE

- 250 g / 8 oz basmati rice
- 25 ml / 1 fl oz sunflower oil
- 100 g / 4 oz onion, diced
- 1 tbsp mustard seeds
- 4 cardamom pods, split and seeds pounded in a pestle and mortar
- 75 g / 3 oz raisins
- 50 g / 2 oz chopped whole almonds
- pinch of saffron threads
- 1 piece fresh fiery red chilli, finely chopped
- 75 g / 3 oz coconut flakes

FOR THE YOGHURT TOPPING

- 500 ml / 1 pint plain yoghurt
- 1 tbsp flaked almonds
- 1½ tsp coconut flakes
- zest of 1 lime
- 1 tbsp raisins

Heat the butter and half the oil and fry the onion over a medium heat for 8–10 minutes or until light brown. Add the cardamom, cumin, ground coriander, ginger, mustard seeds, cloves and finely chopped dried chilli. Fry for a few seconds, then add the crushed garlic and continue to fry for 2 minutes, adding a little water if necessary. Add the potatoes and fry for 8 minutes. Then add the carrots and half the tomatoes which will dissolve to make a sauce.

Add the rest of the oil little by little from this point onwards as you continue to cook the curry. Add the cauliflower florets and continue to cook for 5 minutes, adding more water as you go along (about 150 ml / 6 fl oz each time) to prevent the vegetables from sticking but making sure that it is all absorbed each time to maintain the curry's thick and rich consistency. Then add the saffron, the courgette slices, the coconut butter and tamarind juice and stir until dissolved. Continue to simmer for 20–25 minutes, stirring frequently and adding a little more water as you go. Finally, add the rest of the tomato quarters and the fresh coriander and fold in gently for just a couple of minutes before serving.

Meanwhile, cook the basmati rice according to package directions. In a separate pan, heat the oil and fry the onion until transparent. Add the mustard seeds and crushed cardamom pods and continue to fry for about 8 minutes until pale golden brown. Add the raisins, almonds, saffron threads, finely chopped chilli and coconut flakes and fry for a further 5–6 minutes, stirring regularly. Finally add the cooked rice and stir well so that the flavours mingle and the rice is speckled with the orange hue of the saffron.

To assemble, preheat the oven to 190˚C/375˚F/gas 5. Place the rice at the bottom of an ovenproof dish and then pour the curry over it. Finally pour the yoghurt on top and sprinkle with the almonds, coconut flakes, lime zest and raisins. Heat for 15–20 minutes so that the yoghurt sets slightly. Serve at once.

PIZZAS

When it comes to making bread and pizza doughs, I prefer to remain as old-fashioned and traditional as possible. There is no dried yeast and no food processor for me. I like the frothiness and the unmistakable smell of fresh yeast and the kneading and stretching and general thumping of the dough. But I admit that this is pure romanticism and you could halve the preparation time by resorting to labour-saving devices.

This recipe makes six 10 cm / 4 in pizzas. I prefer my pizza bases thin and crisp so don't allow for a second rising. If you prefer a thicker, more focaccia-like base, you must allow the dough to rise for a further 20 minutes after rolling it out.

I have given three different toppings but the frontiers of possibility are pushed continually further – try lettuce hearts or chicory, Gorgonzola and pears (I had this recently in a pizzeria whose humble location belied the integrity of its menu and the devotion of its Italian staff). By far the most sublime of all is a pizza I ate from a stall in the old Jewish quarter of Rome. It had the thinnest of crispy bases brushed with the sweetest layer of tomato sauce, the creamiest of young buffalo Mozzarella and, to my wonder, the most delicate and delicious layer of courgette flowers, the colour of an Impressionist sunshine. I do not include this recipe here, because unless you are of the rare breed who grow their own flowering courgettes, it is ruinously expensive. Still, if it's the thought that counts, know that a pizza, as well as being a jolly, work-a-day sort of a meal, has aristocratic cousins and start planting the courgette seeds.

SERVES
6

INGREDIENTS

FOR THE DOUGH

- 15 g / ½ oz fresh yeast
- ½ tsp caster sugar
- 150 ml / 6 fl oz hand-hot water
- 300 g / 10 oz strong white flour
- 1 heaped tsp salt
- 1 tbsp virgin olive oil

METHOD

Dissolve the fresh yeast with the sugar in a little of the water and set aside for about 10 minutes until a froth appears on the surface. Place the flour mixed with the salt in a mound on your work top or simply in a bowl and make a shallow well in the centre. Pour the warm liquid into the well and mix with the flour. Then add the olive oil and the rest of the water. It is difficult to give an exact quantity of water so if the dough is too sticky, simply sprinkle a little more flour into it and if it is too dry and does not hold together properly, add a little more water until the dough comes cleanly away from the work surface or bowl. Knead the dough on a lightly floured surface for 8–10 minutes until it is smooth and elastic.

Place in a lightly floured bowl and make an incision across the top with a knife, which will help it rise. Sprinkle a little more flour on top, cover loosely with a tea towel and place in a warm, draught-free spot to rise until doubled in volume. This may take as little as 45 minutes or as long as 3 hours depending on the temperature.

Knock back the dough, adding a little flour if necessary, then knead it briefly – a couple of minutes will do. Divide the dough into 6 even-sized lumps and roll each into 6 rough circles. The dough should not be thicker than 2.5 mm / $\frac{1}{8}$ in thick when rolled out.

INGREDIENTS

FOR THE TOMATO SAUCE
- 500 g / 1 lb ripe tomatoes
- 5 tbsp olive oil
- 75 g / 3 oz onions, diced into 1 cm / $\frac{1}{2}$ in pieces
- 3 cloves garlic, peeled and left whole
- 3 basil leaves

- 1 bay leaf
- pinch of sugar
- 1 tsp sundried tomato purée
- dash of Tabasco
- salt and freshly ground black pepper

METHOD

Blanch the tomatoes in salted boiling water for one minute, until the skins begin to split. Remove from the water and allow to cool. Then remove the skins, scraping away the flesh with a teaspoon to remove the sweet and colourful flesh and chop. Discard the seeds but retain the juices. Heat the olive oil and sweat the onion gently for 2–3 minutes until it is transparent. Add the chopped blanched tomatoes, juice and all, and the remaining ingredients. Bring to the boil for 3–4 minutes and then simmer gently for 30 minutes, stirring regularly. The garlic will go quite soft and sweet and the leaves will infuse the sauce with subtle aromas. When the sauce is well reduced (to about half its original volume) remove from the heat and discard the garlic and herbs.

INGREDIENTS (FOR 6 PIZZA BASES)

TOPPING 1

- 2 red peppers
- 1 yellow pepper
- 6 cloves garlic
- dash of Tabasco
- 1 medium aubergine
- 3 medium courgettes
- 100 g / 4 oz black olives
- 3 small goats' cheeses
- small bunch fresh basil
- 100 ml / 4 fl oz olive oil
- salt and freshly ground black pepper

METHOD

Preheat the oven to 200°C/400°F/gas 6.

Prick each of the pizza bases with a fork, brush generously with tomato sauce and place some of each of the vegetables, including the unpeeled garlic cloves and olives as well as half a goat's cheese, as it is or cut into thick slices on top of each. Drizzle olive oil lightly over the lot, tucking in the basil leaves under the more robust vegetables. Place on a lightly floured baking tray and bake for 15 minutes until the pizza dough is crisp and lightly browned around the edges.

INGREDIENTS (FOR 6 PIZZA BASES)

TOPPING 2

- 135 g / 4½ oz tin artichoke hearts
- 100 ml / 4 fl oz olive oil
- 2 cloves garlic, crushed
- dash of Tabasco
- 500 g / 1 lb baby spinach
- pinch of nutmeg
- 2 medium red onions
- 300 g / 6 oz Feta cheese
- 6 sundried tomatoes in oil, sliced
- 1 heaped tbsp pine nuts
- salt and freshly ground black pepper

METHOD

Preheat the oven to 200°C/400°F/gas 6.

Drain the artichoke hearts and marinate them in the olive oil for an hour or so, adding a little crushed garlic and a dash of Tabasco. Set aside. Meanwhile, sweat the spinach in 1 tbsp olive oil, with the nutmeg, remaining garlic, a pinch of salt and some freshly ground black pepper for 1 minute. Set aside. Peel the red onions and cut into 6 or more wedges. Break the Feta into rough pieces. Prick each of the pizza bases with a fork and brush with tomato sauce. Heap on the vegetables and sundried tomatoes in a generous pile, hiding most of the spinach under the artichokes and red onion. Sprinkle with the Feta and pine nuts. Trickle a little olive oil on top and bake for 15–20 minutes until the edges are golden and crisp.

INGREDIENTS (FOR 6 PIZZA BASES)

TOPPING 3

- 2 medium heads fennel
- 100 ml / 4 fl oz olive oil
- 2 cloves garlic, crushed
- dash of Tabasco
- 2 whole Mozzarella cheeses
- 1 head radicchio
- 3 red onions
- 100 g / 4 oz fresh Parmesan cheese
- salt and freshly ground black pepper

METHOD

Trim the fennel, removing any tough and fibrous ends. Cut into 8 lengthways slices and baste generously with most of the olive oil, a bit of crushed garlic, a dash of Tabasco, salt and pepper. Then slice the Mozzarella, add to the fennel and mix well. Set aside for an hour or more.

Preheat the oven to 200°C/400°F/gas 6. Roughly chop the radicchio and cut the red onion into chunks. Prick each of the pizza bases with a fork and spread over the tomato sauce. Cover first with the radicchio, and lightly season with salt and pepper. Then top with the remaining crushed garlic, the fennel pieces, the red onion and finally the Mozzarella. Drizzle with olive oil and place in the preheated oven for 15–20 minutes until the pizza edges are crisp and golden, the Mozzarella melted and the red onion and fennel charred and softened.

GREEN BEANS WITH RED ONION CONFIT, CANNELLINI BEANS AND TOMATOES

What might be a very typical Mediterranean combination turns Oriental with the addition of teriyaki sauce and ginger. As with most sautéed vegetables, this is delicious with rice – try a robust combination of Italian short-grain, wild rice and Camargue red rice, generously infused with lime and coriander and very finely diced fiery red chilli.

SERVES
4 – 6

INGREDIENTS

- 1 kg / 2 lb green beans
- 250 g / 8 oz firm red tomatoes, quartered
- 250 g / 8 oz cannellini beans (cooked weight)
- 4 tbsp teriyaki sauce
- 1 small piece fresh chilli, diced
- 1 large handful coriander, chopped, reserve some leaves for garnish
- 1 tbsp sesame seeds
- salt and freshly ground black pepper

FOR THE RED ONION CONFIT

- 250 g / 8 oz red onions
- 5 tbsp chilli oil
- ½ tsp soft brown sugar
- 1 piece ginger, about 2.5 cm / 1 in long, grated
- 2 cloves garlic
- dash of Tabasco

METHOD

Top and tail the green beans and blanch in a large pan of salted boiling water for 2–3 minutes, until *al dente*. Immediately refresh under very cold water and set aside.

For the confit, peel the red onions and cut in half along the length, then cut into thin slices, again following the length. Heat half the oil and fry the onion over a gentle heat until soft, gradually adding the sugar, grated ginger, garlic, Tabasco, salt and pepper. The onion will caramelize and you may need to add a drop of water to dislodge any juices that stick to the pan. Transfer to a plate and set aside.

In the same pan, heat the remaining oil and quickly sauté the green beans, adding the tomato quarters for literally 1 minute, turning and tossing the pan in large and dramatic movements (or stir vigorously). Then add the cannellini beans, teriyaki sauce, diced chilli and coriander. Place on a warmed serving plate, and top with the caramelized onion on top. Garnish with more fresh coriander and the sesame seeds.

COUSCOUS
WITH ROASTED VEGETABLES

Couscous is durum wheat and water mixed together and then rolled together to form thousands of tiny balls. It is not, as many people think, a separate kind of grain. Traditionally it is steamed in a couscousier but this can take as long as 1½ hours. However, this quick method yields surprisingly good results. If you wish, serve with a bowl of yoghurt seasoned with garlic, coriander and mint.

SERVES
6

INGREDIENTS

- 500 g / 1 lb couscous
- 750 ml / 1½ pints boiling water
- ½ tsp bouillon powder
- 1 tbsp olive oil
- 1 onion, finely diced
- 1 heaped tsp mustard seeds
- 1 clove garlic, crushed
- salt and freshly ground black pepper

FOR THE VEGETABLES

- 1 red pepper, seeds and pith removed and cut into 6
- 1 yellow pepper, seeds and pith removed and cut into 6
- 1 bulb fennel, trimmed and cut into 6
- 2 medium courgettes, cut into 5 cm / 2 in chunks on the diagonal
- 3 red onions, peeled and cut into 6
- 2 medium aubergines, cut into 5 cm / 2 in chunks
- 3 tbsp olive oil
- dash of Tabasco
- 1 tbsp balsamic vinegar
- 1 clove garlic, crushed
- salt and freshly ground black pepper

METHOD

Preheat the oven to its highest setting.

Place the couscous in a large pan and pour over the boiling water and bouillon powder. The couscous will be soft as soon as the water has been absorbed.

Meanwhile, heat the olive oil and fry the onion until golden brown, adding the mustard seeds, crushed garlic and salt and pepper. Mix with the couscous and set aside.

For the roasted vegetables, mix all the vegetables with the olive oil, Tabasco, balsamic vinegar, garlic and salt and pepper and place in an ovenproof dish. Bake in the preheated oven for 35 minutes or until charred and tender. Serve piled on the couscous.

MASHED POTATO
WITH SAUTEED VEGETABLES

Mashed potatoes as a main course? Why not, especially if they are combined with such elegant partners. The type of mushroom used in the sauce will have a great impact on the final dish and I prefer morels, which are more readily available than in the past. To be sure, cultivated morels do not have the exquisite intensity of wild ones but I would rather have them than none at all.

SERVES
6 – 8

INGREDIENTS

FOR THE MASHED POTATOES
- 4 large potatoes
- 100 g / 4 oz unsalted butter
- salt and white pepper

FOR THE SAUCE
- 100 g / 4 oz butter
- 2 cloves garlic, crushed
- 50 g / 2 oz mushrooms (button, chestnut, chanterelles or morels), thinly sliced
- handful of fresh sorrel, shredded

- handful of fresh chervil
- small bunch chives, finely snipped
- salt and freshly ground black pepper

FOR THE VEGETABLES
- 150 g / 6 oz baby carrots
- 150 g / 6 oz asparagus
- 500 g / 1 lb baby leeks, trimmed and cut on the diagonal
- 150 g / 6 oz broad beans, fresh or frozen, shelled

METHOD

Peel the potatoes and place in a large pan of salted water. Bring to the boil and simmer until tender. Drain and mash with a potato masher and then push through a fine sieve.

If using straightaway, beat in all the butter and adjust seasoning. If not, then beat in 75 g / 3 oz of the butter and refrigerate. To serve, warm the mashed potato in a saucepan, adding the remaining butter.

Separately blanch the carrots, asparagus, leeks and broad beans in plenty of salted boiling water. The vegetables will need 1 minute each, the broad beans 3–4 minutes.

For the sauce, melt the butter and sauté the garlic and mushrooms for 3–4 minutes, adding salt and pepper. Add the vegetables, some of the shredded sorrel, a few sprigs of chervil and half the chives and stir gently so that all the vegetables are coated in the butter. Very gently fold in the broad beans.

Pile the vegetables on top of the mashed potato and garnish with the remaining fresh herbs and with any remaining butter poured over.

CHICKPEA FRITTERS

AND TIKKA SAUCE

These fritters are delicious and the home-made tikka sauce is very simple to make and well worth the effort. Serve with a sautéed green vegetable.

SERVES

6

INGREDIENTS

FOR THE FRITTERS

- 250 g / 8 oz chickpeas, dry weight, soaked overnight in water
- 500 g / 1 lb cooked chickpeas
- 2 tbsp tikka paste
- 1 large red onion, diced
- juice of 1 lime
- 25 g / 1 oz fresh coriander, chopped
- 100 ml / 4 fl oz light olive oil or sunflower oil for frying
- salt and freshly ground black pepper

FOR THE TIKKA PASTE

- 1 heaped tsp dried ginger
- 1 heaped tsp dried coriander

- 1 heaped tsp cumin
- 1 heaped tsp turmeric
- 2 heaped tbsp very red paprika
- ½ tsp dried chilli powder, very red
- 5 tbsp water
- 3 tbsp sunflower oil
- 2–3 cloves garlic, crushed to a smooth paste
- 1 heaped tsp tamarind paste
- ½ large chilli, chopped or blended very finely to form a paste
- 25 g / 1 oz fresh coriander
- 6 tbsp yoghurt

METHOD

To make the fritters, place the raw soaked chickpeas in a food processor and pulverize for 15 seconds until broken down but still gritty in consistency. Mash the cooked chickpeas with a fork or potato masher until almost smooth but with just a few chickpeas nearly whole. Mix with the ground raw chickpeas. Add the tikka paste, red onion, lime juice, fresh coriander and salt and pepper, if required. Mix well and set aside, covered with cling film, for 20 minutes for the flavours to develop.

To make the tikka paste, mix all the spices together and add the water and then the oil. Mix thoroughly. Add the garlic, tamarind, chilli paste and coriander. Mix well and set aside in a covered bowl or jar with a lid. Add the yoghurt just before serving.

Work the fritter mixture with your fingers for a few seconds to make sure it holds together properly and form into rough patties about 7.5 cm / 3 in in diameter and 1 cm / ½ in high. Heat the oil and fry gently for a couple of minutes on both sides until golden brown and crisp. Drain on kitchen paper, then serve hot.

VERMOUTH MUSHROOMS ON TOASTED BRIOCHE

SERVED WITH POACHED EGG

This is a sophisticated dinner party dish to attempt when you are confident about poaching eggs. The trick is to add some clear vinegar to the water and to stir furiously around the egg as soon as you drop it in to keep all the white together. The other trick is to use a simple egg poacher and be done!

SERVES
6

INGREDIENTS

- 75 g / 3 oz butter
- 2 cloves garlic, finely chopped
- 1.25 kg / 2½ lb mixed mushrooms, to include dried (soaked and drained), wild and button
- dash of tamari
- dash of Tabasco
- 3 tbsp vermouth

- 4 tbsp double cream
- 6 slices home-made brioche (see page 247)
- 1 tbsp clear vinegar
- 6 eggs, size 3
- 250 g / 8 oz fresh baby spinach
- salt and freshly ground black pepper

METHOD

Melt the butter in a frying pan and sauté the garlic over a low heat for a few minutes, making sure it does not burn. Add the mushrooms, tamari, Tabasco and salt and pepper and sauté for a further 3–4 minutes until they are tender and release their liquor. Add the vermouth and reduce to about half, then add the cream and stir. Remove from heat and set aside.

Toast the slices of brioche under a grill until they are golden brown. Remove and cover with a cloth to keep warm.

Bring a pan of salted water to the boil, add the vinegar and carefully break in one egg at a time. Stir all the time with a fork and as soon as the yolk is set to your liking remove the egg to a plate, using a slotted spoon. Repeat with the other eggs.

Gently reheat the mushrooms and stir in the spinach so that it just wilts. Immediately remove from heat.

Serve a slice of toasted brioche topped with a poached egg and surrounded with the mushrooms and spinach with sauce spooned all around.

CANNELLONI

There is no comparison between cannelloni made with dried pasta tubes and those you make yourself with fresh lasagne sheets. There is no need to blanch the spinach. It can simply wilt in the heat.

SERVES
4 – 6
12 ROLLS

INGREDIENTS

- thick tomato sauce (see page 100)
- 350 g / 12 oz fresh spinach, washed
- scraping of fresh nutmeg
- 1 tsp olive oil
- ½ small red onion, diced
- 100 g / 4 oz chestnut mushrooms, sliced
- 2 cloves garlic, crushed
- 1 tsp tamari
- 250 g / 8 oz Ricotta
- 25 g / 1 oz Parmesan cheese, grated
- 250 g / 8 oz fresh spinach pasta sheets, cut into 3 strips, each 8 cm / 3½ in wide and 36 cm / 16 in long
- 250 g / 8 oz Smetana
- 250 g / 8 oz Mascarpone cheese
- 100 g / 4 oz Cheddar cheese, grated
- salt and freshly ground black pepper

METHOD

Preheat the oven to 200°C/400°F/gas 6.

Place the spinach and a little salt and pepper in a pan set over a low heat for 1 minute until wilted. Drain thoroughly and add a little grated nutmeg. Chop roughly and set aside to cool.

Heat the olive oil and when it is very hot, add first the onion and sauté for 5–6 minutes, then add the sliced mushrooms, crushed garlic and tamari. Sauté for 1–2 minutes until browned. Mix with the spinach and set aside to cool. Then mix with the Ricotta and Parmesan.

To assemble the cannelloni, lay a strip of pasta on a dry chopping board and place a heaped tablespoon of the filling at one end of the strip. Bring the outer end over and roll to make a tube with very little overlap. Trim the ends with a sharp knife and proceed in this way until all the pasta sheets and filling are used up.

Place half the tomato sauce in an ovenproof dish and arrange the cannelloni side by side in two lines. Cover with the remaining tomato sauce and then with the Smetana and Mascarpone. Finally add the grated cheese and bake in the preheated oven for 25–30 minutes until golden brown.

FILLED AUBERGINE ROLLS

Slices of potatoes, red onion and tomatoes (see page 63) laid out on a plate in a circle make an attractive backdrop for these aubergine rolls, drizzled with a little olive oil and pesto. The smoked Fontina cheese and the rich nature of aubergine make this a deeply flavoured dish.

(see page 63)

SERVES
6

INGREDIENTS

- 3 medium aubergines, cut in half and flesh scooped out to within 5 mm / ¼ in of the skin
- 150 ml / 6 fl oz olive oil
- dash of Tabasco
- 500 g / 1 lb tomatoes, blanched, skinned, deseeded and chopped
- 3 cloves garlic, crushed
- 1 tbsp balsamic vinegar
- 100 ml / 4 fl oz water
- ½ small head fennel, chopped
- 2 large courgettes, diced
- 450 g / 14 oz tin kidney beans, including half their preserving liquid
- 50 g / 2 oz pesto
- 50 g / 2 oz smoked Fontina cheese, very finely sliced
- several leaves basil, for garnish
- salt and freshly ground black pepper

METHOD

Preheat the oven to 220°C/425°F/gas 7.

Brush the scooped out aubergine halves with a little olive oil, salt, pepper and Tabasco. Bake in the preheated oven for about 40 minutes until the remaining flesh is completely soft.

Meanwhile, chop the aubergine flesh and fry in half the remaining olive oil, with the chopped tomatoes which will release liquid into the pan plus the crushed garlic and the balsamic vinegar. Stir often and add water, a little at a time, as the aubergine sticks to the pan. The aubergine will be soft in about 30 minutes. Remove from the pan and set aside.

Add the chopped fennel to the same still hot pan, adding only a touch of oil and water if you need to. A minute later, add the courgette and sauté for a further minute or two. Finally, return the fried aubergine to the pan and mix well, adding the tinned kidney beans and juice too.

Lightly baste the aubergine halves with pesto and line each with a thin slice of smoked Fontina cheese. Then fill with the vegetable mixture and roll. The two ends will meet in the middle and need to be secured with 3 cocktail sticks. Brush with the rest of the pesto. Pour the remaining olive oil in an ovenproof dish and pack the aubergine rolls tightly together. Bake for 15 minutes, until the pesto crisps up a little. Serve hot, garnished with the basil.

CHEESE AND ONION BREAD PUDDING

This is as down-to-earth and filling as it sounds and the kind of dish everyone secretly loves. You can make it more sophisticated by replacing the Cheddar with a smoked Fontina cheese and replacing up to half the milk with double cream, and you could also wilt some baby spinach or rocket into the egg mixture. Other vegetables such as sautéed courgettes and mushrooms are equally successful. But here is the recipe in its basic form and you can ring the changes for yourself.

SERVES
6

INGREDIENTS

- 25 g / 1 oz unsalted butter plus 15 g / ½ oz to butter the dish
- 3 large onions, finely sliced
- 1 tsp fresh thyme leaves
- 2 cloves garlic, finely crushed (optional)
- 50 g / 2 oz grated Parmesan cheese

- 150 g / 6 oz grated Cheddar cheese
- 1 tbsp fresh chives, finely snipped
- 8 slices wholemeal bread, crusts removed
- 3 eggs, size 3
- 500 ml / 1 pint milk
- salt and freshly ground black pepper

METHOD

Preheat the oven to 190°C/375°F/gas 5.

Heat the butter in a frying pan and fry the onion for 10–15 minutes until soft and golden brown. Add the fresh thyme, the garlic if using and season with salt and pepper. Combine the Parmesan with the Cheddar and finely snipped chives, then mix with the fried onion.

Place half the bread slices in a buttered ovenproof dish, trimming the slices if necessary so that they fit snugly. Cover with half the cheese and onion mixture. Repeat with the remaining bread and finish with the cheese mixture.

Place the eggs and milk in a bowl and whisk. Season with salt and pepper, taking into account the saltiness of the cheese. Pour over the bread and cheese and place in the preheated oven for 30–35 minutes until the custard is set, moist and golden brown. Serve straight from the oven.

VEGETABLE BROCHETTES

WITH SPICED RICE

Almost any kind of vegetable can be skewered onto wooden or metal sticks, marinated in any manner of seasoning and left to roast over hot coals or under ordinary grills. Even a vegetable as hard as pumpkin can feature on a brochette, as can papaya and mango, patty pan, chicory and fennel to name but a few. Experiment to your heart's content. You may wish to offer a variety of brochettes at the same time, keeping the longer cooking vegetables on one stick and the faster cooking ones on another. But even mixing them is wonderful, with some vegetables completely soft and others still firm. Make cuts into the flesh of tougher vegetables to help them absorb the spices and herbs of the marinade. Dip a pastry brush lusciously into the sauce and spread generously over each vegetable or place in a large bowl with the sauce poured on top. The *mélange* suggested in this recipe is daring, the striking colour and sweetness of some marrying with the bitterness of others.

INGREDIENTS

- 8 baby aubergines
- 8 baby courgettes
- 500 g / 1 lb small pumpkin, unpeeled
- 1 papaya
- 1 red pepper
- 16 thick asparagus spears
- 4 heads chicory
- 8 shallots
- 8 tomatoes
- 16 yellow and green patty pans
- 100 g / 4 oz shiitake mushrooms
- 100 g / 4 oz oyster mushrooms

FOR THE MARINADE

- 150 ml / 6 fl oz olive oil
- 4 tbsp tamari
- 1 tbsp Tabasco
- 1 tbsp grain mustard
- 1 heaped tsp cumin
- 1 tbsp paprika
- juice of 1½ limes
- 2 cloves garlic, crushed
- 1 red chilli, finely chopped

FOR THE RICE
- 500 g / 1 lb Italian short-grain brown rice
- 1 litre / 2 pints water
- salt
- 2 red peppers
- 150 g / 6 oz courgette

- 1 large carrot
- 1 fine leek
- 1 corn on the cob
- 1 heaped tbsp finely chopped parsley
- 1 heaped tbsp finely chopped coriander
- several sprigs very fresh coriander, to garnish

METHOD

Mix all the marinade ingredients together and allow the flavours to mingle for as long as you can – a good hour is ideal.

Meanwhile prepare the vegetables. Leave all the baby vegetables whole – you do not even need to remove the stalks. Cut the pumpkin and papaya into slices about 2.5 cm / 1 in wide and 10 cm / 4 in long. Leave the skin on both. Cut the red pepper into 6 large strips. Choose fat, juicy asparagus spears, trimmed to about 12.5 cm / 5 in long. Remove any brown leaves from the chicory and cut into quarters. Blanch the shallots in boiling water for 1 minute and then peel. Wash the tomatoes, but leave whole. Make shallow incisions into all vegetables except the tomatoes and mushrooms.

Place all the brochette vegetables in a shallow dish and pour over half the marinade. Mix well, cover and leave to marinate for at least one hour or overnight.

Place the rice in a pressure cooker with the lightly salted water. Bring to pressure, then reduce heat and cook for 15 minutes. Remove from heat but do not remove lid for a further 5 minutes.

Meanwhile, prepare the vegetables for the rice. Remove all seeds and pith from the peppers and slice into the thinnest and longest possible slivers, not unlike noodles. Repeat with the courgette, carrot and leek. Slice the corn kernels off the sides of the cob. Then heat the reserved marinade in a wok or large pan. First add the carrots, seconds later, the leek, then the corn, finally the pepper and courgette. Sauté on a high heat for a minute, taking care not to burn either the marinade or vegetables and retaining the redness of the paprika throughout. Remove half the vegetables and set aside. Immediately add the rice to those left in the pan and continue to sauté for 2 minutes, stirring all the time until the rice is hot. Remove from heat and immediately add the chopped parsley and coriander. Taste and add more salt, Tabasco and lime juice if you wish. Set aside and keep warm.

Preheat the grill. Skewer the vegetables onto large sticks – metal ones are best and won't burn under the intense heat. Brush with the marinade and place under the hot grill for about 15 minutes, turning over at least once and removing only when all the vegetables are charred and sizzling on all sides.

Heap the rice onto a large plate and stack the brochettes on top, scattering generously with the remaining vegetable slivers and coriander.

NOODLES WITH SAUTEED AUBERGINE AND SMOKED TOFU

This recipe again combines Oriental and Mediterranean influences. It is aromatic and a good base for some of the vegetable dishes such as grilled shiitake mushrooms with spring onions (see page 166) and is perfect followed by a baked fruit dessert.

SERVES
6

INGREDIENTS

- 5 tbsp olive oil mixed with 1 tbsp sesame oil (optional)
- 2 large aubergines, sliced into 5 mm / ¼ in slices, then into thin strips
- 2 tbsp balsamic vinegar
- 3 cloves garlic, crushed
- 3 tbsp sesame seeds
- 1 piece fresh chilli, very finely chopped, with a little reserved for garnish

- 2 tbsp coriander, roughly chopped, half reserved for garnish
- 125 g / 5 oz smoked tofu, cut into thin strips
- 1 tbsp tamari
- dash of Tabasco
- 500 g / 1 lb thick egg noodles
- 15 g / ½ oz chives, finely snipped, for garnish
- salt and freshly ground black pepper

METHOD

Heat three-quarters of the oil in a pan and, over a high heat, sauté the strips of aubergine with the balsamic vinegar and the crushed garlic. The aubergine strips should shrivel and shrink, become golden brown but still retain a slightly chewy texture. If they dry and stick to the pan, simply add a little water to loosen the juices from the bottom of the pan and continue until evaporated. Continue for 5–6 minutes until the aubergine is browned. At the last moment, add 1 tbsp sesame seeds and continue to sauté for a few minutes until they begin to split and pop and generally jump about. Then add the chilli and coriander and remove from heat. Set aside. In the same pan, heat the remaining oil and sauté the tofu strips, this time with the addition of the tamari and Tabasco. Again, toss and turn until the tofu goes brown and begins to crisp in places, also adding 1 tbsp sesame seeds and frying as before.

Meanwhile, bring a large pan of salted water to the boil and cook the noodles for 4 minutes or according to packet instructions. Drain and mix with the aubergine and tofu. Arrange individual servings by twisting the noodles around a fork and heaping onto the plates and garnish with the remaining sesame seeds, chilli, chives and coriander.

POLENTA GNOCCHI
WITH ROASTED VEGETABLES

This is my favourite way of eating polenta. At Cranks, we serve the polenta in triangular pieces, laid out on a large and colourful dish laden with all kinds of roasted or grilled vegetables.

SERVES

6

INGREDIENTS

- 1 litre / 2 pints milk or water
- 150 g / 6 oz butter
- 350 g / 12 oz polenta
- 3 egg yolks
- 100 g / 4 oz Parmesan cheese, grated
- pinch of nutmeg (optional)
- 15 g / ½ oz basil, finely shredded
- salt and freshly ground black pepper

FOR THE VEGETABLES

- 2 bulbs fennel, cut lengthways into 6
- 1 red pepper, cut into 6 long strips
- 1 yellow pepper, cut into 6 long strips
- 3 small red onions, cut into quarters
- 1 large aubergine, cut into 5 cm / 2 in chunks
- 3 medium courgettes, cut on the slant into thick slices
- 2 bulbs garlic, separated but left unpeeled
- 100 ml / 4 fl oz olive oil
- dash of Tabasco
- 6 tomatoes, left whole
- salt and freshly ground black pepper

METHOD

For the gnocchi, heat the milk or water with a pinch of salt and a knob of butter. When it boils, pour in the polenta in a continuous stream and stir vigorously to avoid lumps forming. Simmer gently for 15–20 minutes, stirring regularly.

Remove from heat and add the egg yolks, half the Parmesan and the nutmeg if using. Pour the mixture onto a smooth board or work surface that has been slightly dampened. Smooth the mixture down so it is of equal thickness all over. Allow to cool, then cut out circles 5 cm / 2 in in diameter with a pastry cutter.

Preheat the oven to 200°C/400°F/gas 6. Butter an ovenproof dish and arrange the gnocchi so that they slightly overlap. Melt the remaining butter, pour over the polenta and place in the oven for 20–25 minutes until golden brown. Remove from oven and sprinkle with the remaining Parmesan and basil.

For the vegetables, preheat the oven to its highest setting. Place all the vegetables except the tomatoes in a dish with most of the oil, a little Tabasco and salt and pepper. Place in the oven and bake for 35–40 minutes until all the vegetables are charred and slightly shrivelled. Add the tomatoes about halfway through the cooking time, making sure that they are basted in olive oil. Place the polenta on a serving platter and pile the vegetables on top. Serve at once.

FILLED BAKED POTATOES

Here is a simple, warming meal in the hand with an infinite possibility of fillings which you can make as grand or simple as you like. Simply oil the skins first to avoid their otherwise rather awful dullness. Or use smaller potatoes and make more than one filling at a time and you can enjoy them all at one sitting.

SERVES

6

INGREDIENTS

- 6 large baking potatoes or 12 smaller ones, baked in their jackets

FILLING 1

- 100 g / 4 oz button mushrooms, thickly sliced
- 1 tbsp olive oil
- dash of Tabasco
- 1 tbsp tamari
- 1 egg, size 3, beaten
- 15 g / ½ oz butter
- 150 g / 6 oz Cheddar or Red Leicester cheese, grated
- 100 ml / 4 fl oz sour cream

- 2 tsp grain mustard
- 2 tsp snipped chives
- 1 clove garlic, crushed
- salt and freshly ground black pepper

FILLING 2

- 1 egg, size 3, beaten
- 75 g / 3 oz black olives, roughly chopped
- 100 g / 4 oz Mozzarella cheese, grated
- 1 clove garlic, crushed
- 4 sundried tomatoes in oil, cut into thin slivers
- handful of fresh basil, finely shredded
- salt and freshly ground black pepper

METHOD

Preheat the oven to 180°C/350°F/gas 4. Oil the potatoes and bake for 45 minutes or until soft.

FILLING 1

Sauté the mushrooms in a little olive oil and season with a dash of Tabasco, tamari and salt and pepper. Cut tops from the potatoes and scoop out the flesh with a spoon, leaving a shell 1 cm / ½ in thick. Place the potato flesh in a bowl and mix with the mushrooms, beaten egg, butter, grated cheese, sour cream, mustard, chives, crushed garlic and salt and pepper. Scoop this back into the potatoes and bake at 180°C/350°F/gas 4 for 10–15 minutes.

FILLING 2

Proceed as above, mixing the potato with the egg, olives, Mozzarella, crushed garlic, sundried tomatoes, basil, salt and pepper. Bake as before.

WILD MUSHROOM FRICASSEE

There are now so many different varieties of mushrooms available at supermarkets and specialist suppliers that there is barely an excuse to settle for the tasteless polystyrene lookalikes. Oyster mushrooms, which have taken better than most to cultivation, are a tame equivalent of their originals, if you are to judge by their size. On the Suffolk coast, I have picked them 1 foot in diameter, cleaned and cooked them in nothing more than butter, garlic, white wine and salt and pepper. Delicious.

Use as many varieties as you can and always supplement with mixed dried mushrooms, which often contain some pieces of the rare and astronomically expensive morels and always have the depth of flavour required for a dish like this one. Adding a touch of tamari and brandy to the hot soaking water brings out the flavour. Also take great care in cleaning the fresh mushrooms, especially the chanterelles, and in ridding them of their grit by wiping gently with kitchen paper or use a small soft brush. Do not wash them in water. Serve this with the Individual Soufflés on page 93 for an extravagant meal.

Serve this with the Individual Soufflés on page 93 for an extravagant meal.

SERVES

6

INGREDIENTS

- 125 g / 5 oz dried assorted wild mushrooms
- 500 ml / 1 pint hot water to soak mushrooms
- 1 tbsp tamari
- 1 tbsp brandy
- 2 cloves garlic, crushed
- ½ tsp grain mustard
- 40 g / 1½ oz butter
- ¼ tsp soft brown sugar
- 2 large sprigs fresh tarragon
- 100 g / 4 oz shiitake mushrooms, tough ends removed, cut into thick slivers
- 125 g / 5 oz oyster mushrooms
- 125 g / 5 oz chanterelles, carefully cleaned
- 2 spring onions, finely sliced
- 150 g / 6 oz baby spinach
- 1 tbsp double cream
- salt and freshly ground black pepper

METHOD

Soak the dried mushrooms in the hot water together with the tamari and brandy. Strain through a sieve lined with muslin and return to the liquid. Then place in a large frying pan and bring to the boil together with the crushed garlic, mustard and butter, stirring continuously. Then add the sugar which simply rounds off the taste. Add the whole sprigs of tarragon and continue to stir occasionally as the juices reduce to about half their original volume.

Add the trimmed shiitake mushrooms cut into thick slivers and simmer for a couple of minutes, then carefully fold in and cook the oyster mushrooms for just a minute. Then, again very carefully, add the chanterelles. Remove the wilted sprigs of tarragon. One minute later add the spring onion and the baby spinach until it just wilts. Remove from heat and stir in the double cream and season to taste. Serve with the individual soufflés. The fricassée is also brilliant with pasta, simply served on toast or as a luxurious filling for fluffy omelettes.

INDIVIDUAL SOUFFLES

These are based on Delia Smith's twice-baked soufflés, but I have replaced the Cheddar with Gruyère and the grain mustard with shredded sorrel, but you could use both. I've also added a whole garlic clove to infuse the milk along with the onion. If sorrel is unavailable, you could try spinach or rocket. Serve with the mushroom fricassée on page 91.

Serve with the mushroom fricassée on page 91.

SERVES

4

INGREDIENTS

- 450 ml / 16 fl oz milk
- 1 large onion, halved
- 1 clove garlic, left whole
- 6–7 whole peppercorns
- 50 g / 2 oz unsalted butter
- 50 g / 2 oz self-raising flour

- 4 eggs, size 3, separated
- 1–2 leaves sorrel, finely shredded
- pinch of freshly ground nutmeg
- 250 g / 8 oz Gruyère cheese, grated
- salt

METHOD

Butter 4 x 150 ml / 6 fl oz ramekins. Preheat the oven to 180°C/350°F/gas 4.

Bring the milk to simmering point with the halved onion, garlic clove, the peppercorns and a little salt. Strain.

Make a roux by melting the butter and adding the flour, stirring all the time until both are well amalgamated and leave the sides of the pan clean. Gradually add the milk, stirring the whole time and cook gently for 2 minutes. Transfer to mixing bowl and cool slightly.

Meanwhile, whisk the egg whites until stiff and set aside. Beat the egg yolks, sorrel and nutmeg into the cooled sauce. Fold in three-quarters of the cheese and the whisked egg whites. Pour into the prepared ramekins.

Place the ramekins in a shallow ovenproof dish and fill with hot water reaching halfway up the sides of the ramekins. Bake for 15 minutes, then remove from the oven and set aside. At this point, the soufflés can be left for several hours.

For the second baking, turn out the soufflés onto a baking sheet, sprinkle with the remaining cheese and bake at 200°C/400°F/gas 6 for 20 minutes. Serve immediately.

FILLED GIANT PUMPKIN
WITH HERBED WHIPPED CREAM

If ever there was a convivial main course to serve among friends, this is it. I have made Raymond Blanc's version in which he serves pumpkin soup in its own shell, loved the ingenuity of it and wanted for a long time to come up with a version of my own. This is it.

SERVES
6 – 8

INGREDIENTS

- 1 pumpkin, approximately 1.25 kg / 3 lb, top reserved and seeds removed
- 3 tbsp olive oil
- 1 tbsp tamari
- 1 tbsp red wine or brandy
- dash of Tabasco
- 1 clove garlic, crushed

FOR THE HERBED WHIPPED CREAM
- 500 ml / 1 pint whipping cream
- 1 bunch coriander, finely chopped
- juice of ½ lime
- 1 clove garlic, crushed
- 1 small piece chilli, very finely chopped
- salt and freshly ground black pepper

FOR THE FILLING
- 4 medium carrots, cut into chunks
- 4 medium parsnips, cut into chunks
- 2 bulbs fennel, cut into wedges
- 4 tbsp olive oil
- 4 medium courgettes
- 500 g / 1 lb baby onions
- 25 g / 1 oz butter or extra olive oil
- 1 tbsp soft brown sugar
- 6–8 garlic cloves, unpeeled
- 50 g / 2 oz whole almonds, blanched and skins removed
- salt and freshly ground black pepper

METHOD

To make the filling, preheat the oven to its highest setting. Place the carrots, parsnips and fennel on a baking tray and baste with most of the olive oil. Baste the courgettes with the remaining oil and place in a separate tray. Roast the carrots, fennel and parsnips 30–35 minutes until well browned, but remember that they will be returned to the oven for a further 10 minutes so don't over-roast. Do the same with the courgettes, but bake for only 25 minutes. Remove from the oven and set aside.

To bake the pumpkin, lower the oven temperature to 150°C/300°F/gas 2. Make 7 or 8 skin-deep slits on the outside to prevent the pumpkin from splitting during cooking. Also make a few criss-cross cuts on the inside so that the pumpkin flesh can better absorb the seasoning.

Mix the olive oil, tamari, red wine or brandy, Tabasco and crushed garlic and brush all over the inside of the pumpkin, making sure it gets right into the flesh. Wrap the pumpkin in foil and bake in the preheated oven for 50–60 minutes until tender but not too soft. Remove the foil and increase the oven temperature to maximum for 10 minutes so the flesh can caramelize slightly.

Meanwhile, place the unpeeled baby onions in a pan of boiling water for 1 minute to loosen the skins slightly. Drain, peel and return to the same pan with the butter and sugar. Add 150 ml / 6 fl oz water (or enough to cover the onions) and cover with a lid. Bring to the boil, then simmer for about 25 minutes, adding more water if necessary and cooking until the onions are soft and caramelized.

Meanwhile, make the herbed cream by lightly whipping the cream and gently folding in all the other ingredients. Set aside.

Return the roasted carrots and courgettes to the oven to heat through while the pumpkin is undergoing its final 10 minutes' cooking. Mix the carrots, parsnips, fennel and courgettes together with the glazed onions and almonds, season to taste and fill the pumpkin with the mixture. Serve with the herbed cream sauce on the side.

NOTE

A quicker filling can be made by simply blanching the carrots and fennel for 2 minutes, adding to the glazed onions and the courgettes and continuing to sauté for 5–6 minutes until tender and well coated in the onion juices.

MIDDLE EASTERN POTATO CASSEROLE

A dish of this simplicity depends entirely on slow cooking so that the flavours have plenty of time to develop.

INGREDIENTS

- 1.75 kg / 3½ lb potatoes
- 750 g / 1½ lb onions, diced
- 50 ml / 2 fl oz olive oil
- 1 tsp turmeric
- 1 tsp ground coriander
- 65 ml / 2½ fl oz water
- dash of Tabasco

- 3 cloves garlic, crushed
- 4–5 strands saffron, dissolved in 50 ml / 2 fl oz hot water
- 150 g /6 oz raisins
- 1 tbsp fresh parsley
- 1 tbsp fresh coriander
- salt and freshly ground black pepper

METHOD

Peel and cut the potatoes into even-sized pieces and place in a pan of cold, salted water. Bring to the boil until tender but still firm, as they are going to cook further. Drain and set aside.

Fry the onion in the olive oil until transparent and add the turmeric and ground coriander. Continue to fry until the spices are well absorbed and the grittiness is all cooked out. Add the potatoes and half the water. Add the salt, pepper, Tabasco and crushed garlic and simmer for a further 7–8 minutes. Now add the saffron stock and raisins and continue to simmer for at least another 10 minutes, until the potatoes are tender and the sauce is thickened and a rich golden colour with the flavours mingled into an evocative whiff of the orient.

Just before serving, add in the chopped parsley and coriander and, if you wish, a further glug of olive oil, gently stirred in.

SPAGHETTI
WITH RADICCHIO

The sweet, soft flesh of freshly roasted garlic – this time wrapped in foil to preserve the sweetness and to avoid browning – adds further depth to the dish but it is as simple and elegant as a pasta can be. You could use a linguine or tagliatelle for this dish. I made it with spaghetti simply because I wanted to add a little sophistication to this most prosaic pasta. Serve with a large portion of spinach lightly sautéed and tossed in butter or olive oil with nothing but salt and freshly ground pepper for seasoning.

SERVES

6

INGREDIENTS

- 6 cloves garlic
- 2–3 heads radicchio
- 1 tbsp olive oil
- 750 g / 1½ lb spaghetti
- 50 g / 2 oz butter

- 1 tsp grain mustard
- 500 ml / 1 pint double cream
- Parmesan cheese, to serve
- salt and freshly ground black pepper

METHOD

Preheat the oven to 220°C/425°F/gas 7. Wrap the garlic loosely in a piece of foil and bake for about 20 minutes or until soft. Allow to cool slightly and scoop out the flesh.

Meanwhile, separate the radicchio leaves, rinse gently and dry in a salad spinner or between two clean tea towels. Bunch the leaves together, chop roughly and set aside.

Bring a large pan of salted boiling water to the boil, add the olive oil to prevent the pasta from sticking and immediately add the pasta, holding it all as a big bunch in your hand and lowering it gently into the water as it begins to soften. Reduce the heat so that the water does not boil over and stir the pasta a couple of times at the beginning with a fork to separate out the long strands.

Meanwhile, melt the butter in a large saucepan over a low heat and add the radicchio, tossing and turning for just 1 minute so it wilts but retains as much of its colour as possible. Remove from the heat.

When the pasta is *al dente*, run briefly under cold water to remove the excess starch and immediately add to the pan with the radicchio. Add the garlic flesh, the grain mustard and the double cream. Season with salt and pepper and gently bring to the boil, slowly turning the pasta over all the time. Serve immediately with Parmesan.

SOUBISE RICE

This is a kind of risotto made with long-grain rice instead of Italian, short rounded rice. Unlike classical risotto, it is not stirred during cooking but left to absorb the wine and stock as it gently simmers. I've added fennel to the onion for an even sweeter, more delicate flavour and, if you wish, add sautéed mushrooms or spinach towards the end of the cooking time.

You could also serve it straight from the pan, simply garnished with fresh herbs, rather than bake it with breadcrumbs but this does give it a homely feel which makes it perfect for family meals.

SERVES
4 – 6

INGREDIENTS

- 65 g / 2½ oz butter
- 600 g / 1¼ lb onions, diced
- 2 cloves garlic, finely chopped (optional)
- 1 bulb fennel, chopped into 1 cm / ½ in dice
- 500 g / 1 lb Basmati rice
- 150 ml / 6 fl oz dry white wine
- 350 ml / 12 fl oz hot light vegetable stock

- 1 bay leaf
- 75 g / 3 oz fresh Parmesan cheese
- 50 ml / 2 fl oz double cream
- 125 g / 5 oz fresh white breadcrumbs
- 1 bunch fresh chives, snipped very small
- salt and freshly ground black pepper

METHOD

Melt the butter in a pan and cook the onion and garlic gently, with the lid on, for about 30 minutes, adding the fennel about halfway through, until tender but not browned.

Add the rice and stir for 10 minutes. Pour in the wine and hot stock together with salt and the bay leaf. Bring to a simmer, stir and then cover the pan and cook for 15–20 minutes until the liquid is absorbed and the rice is tender. Remove the bay leaf and stir in the Parmesan and double cream.

Preheat the oven to 200°C/400°F/gas 6. Lightly butter an ovenproof dish and fill with the rice mixture. Sprinkle the breadcrumbs mixed with the chives over the rice and bake in the preheated oven for 15 minutes until the breadcrumbs are a pale golden colour. Serve with a green salad and steamed broccoli tossed in olive oil and grain mustard.

LASAGNE

Poor old lasagne – what a part of the British culinary institution, yet how maligned and how derided it has become. Lasagne appears in its various guises in vegetarian as well as non-vegetarian restaurants throughout the land. Every supermarket chilled and frozen cabinet boasts at least one example. It has become almost a joke dish, the last refuge for soggy pasta and overcooked vegetables floating in watery and undercooked sauces. But here is an example of lasagne with all its many layers of many colours, still warming and rich, but light and modern too.

INGREDIENTS

- 10–12 sheets fresh lasagne, preferably spinach
- 150 ml / 6 fl oz sour cream or crème fraîche
- 250 g / 8 oz smoked Fontina cheese or another hard cheese such as Cheddar or Gruyère

TOMATO SAUCE
- 1 medium onion, diced
- 25 ml / 1 fl oz olive oil
- 500 g / 1 lb whole, peeled tinned tomatoes
- 2 cloves garlic, finely sliced
- 1 large handful basil, reserve some whole leaves
- salt and freshly ground black pepper

FILLING 1
- 500 g / 1 lb petit pois
- 50 g / 2 oz butter
- 500 g / 1 lb fennel, trimmed and cut into 2.5 cm / 1 in chunks

- 1 clove garlic, finely sliced
- 1 tbsp plain flour
- 100 ml / 4 fl oz double cream
- salt and freshly ground black pepper

FILLING 2
- 25 ml / 1 fl oz olive oil
- 1 large aubergine, cut into 2. 5 cm / 1 in chunks
- 1 clove garlic
- dash of Tabasco

FILLING 3
- 500 g / 1 lb spinach, washed and stalks removed
- pinch of nutmeg
- 1 clove garlic, crushed
- 2 tbsp Greek yoghurt or crème fraîche or sour cream
- salt and freshly ground black pepper

M E T H O D

First make the tomato sauce. Heat the oil, then add the onion and fry until transparent, then add the tinned tomatoes and crush with a wooden spoon to make smaller pieces, and the finely sliced garlic. Add the basil, salt and pepper and cook gently for about 25 minutes until all the water has evaporated and the sauce is thick. Remove the cooked basil and replace with some freshly chopped leaves.

In the meantime, make *Filling 1*. Blanch the petits pois in boiling salted water for 5 minutes and refresh under cold water. Melt the butter in a saucepan and gently sauté the fennel and garlic until tender. Add the petits pois, mix well and sprinkle the flour on top. Stir thoroughly until it is well absorbed, season and then add the double cream to make a rich sauce for the fennel and peas. Set aside.

For *Filling 2*, heat the olive oil and sauté the aubergine pieces with the garlic and Tabasco until they are browned and tender. Set aside.

Finally, for *Filling 3*, wilt the spinach in a saucepan placed over a medium heat in only the water which may be clinging to it for no more than a minute. Immediately strain off any excess liquid and season lightly with nutmeg, salt and pepper and a little crushed garlic. Add the Greek yoghurt, sour cream or crème fraîche and set aside.

Preheat the oven to 200°C/400°F/gas 6. Place a generous layer of the tomato sauce in the bottom of an oval ovenproof dish, then a layer of pasta sheets, trimmed to fit if necessary. Then alternate layers of each of the filling mixtures, with pasta sheets in between until all fillings and pasta are used up. Finish off with a layer of tomato sauce, which will be the most liquid of all fillings and which must completely cover the pasta so that it does not dry out. Spread with the sour cream or crème fraîche. Finally, add the grated cheese on top and bake in the preheated oven for 25–30 minutes until the cheese is brown and melted and bubbling.

POTATO GALETTE

WITH BABY VEGETABLES IN SAFFRON, THYME, LIME AND CHILLI BUTTER

This is most definitely sophisticated enough for a dinner party or other special occasion. Potatoes, when they are waxy, such as the French Charlotte potatoes, and cooked slowly are very different indeed to the common baking or boiling potatoes and especially here as they take on the orange hue and the pungent, earthy, even slightly bitter aroma of saffron. Spanish La Mancha saffron is by far the best and worth treating yourself to. Buy the filaments rather than the powder and keep them in a cool, dark, dry place. You may wish to use only saffron in this recipe and omit the turmeric altogether.

If you cannot find purple broccoli which has a fairly short season, you can use green or replace altogether with another green vegetable such as green beans. This dish can be served in an informal fashion with the potatoes in one dish and the baby vegetables and chanterelles in another, but for a smarter presentation, place slices of potatoes in concentric rings on individual warmed plates and pile the vegetables in the centre in a delicate mound.

INGREDIENTS

SERVES

6

- 1.5 kg / 3 lb waxy potatoes
- 100 ml / 4 fl oz olive oil
- 50 ml / 2 fl oz water
- 2 cloves garlic, finely sliced
- handful of fresh basil leaves
- 1 tsp turmeric (optional) or replace with extra saffron
- 6–7 strands saffron
- salt and freshly ground black pepper

FOR THE VEGETABLES
- pinch of saffron strands
- 300 g / 10 oz baby carrots with their leaves left on

- 100 g / 4 oz purple broccoli
- 100 g / 4 oz fine asparagus spears
- 100 g / 4 oz butter
- 2 cloves garlic, finely chopped
- dash of Tabasco
- small bunch of chives, finely snipped, or 1 tbsp fresh thyme leaves, left whole
- juice of ½ lime
- 1 small piece fresh chilli, very finely chopped
- 150 g / 6 oz chanterelle mushrooms
- 1 tsp tamari (optional)
- salt and freshly ground black pepper

METHOD

Preheat the oven to 200°C/400°F/gas 6.

Peel the potatoes and preferably slice thinly by hand so they leak out less water, although for a very even finish you may wish to use a food processor set on a 5 mm / ⅛ in blade. Pat the slices dry between two clean tea towels. Then mix with the olive oil, water and all the seasonings. Place in an ovenproof dish covered with a lid or in a dish covered with aluminium foil. Bake in the preheated oven for 1 hour by which time the potatoes will have softened but retained their shape and texture. They will also have turned a lovely yellow. Remove from the heat before they go brown or begin to crisp.

Meanwhile, prepare the vegetables. First, soak a good pinch of saffron filaments in a couple of tablespoons of hot water and set aside for 10–15 minutes.

Lightly scrape the skin of the carrots (this is optional), then trim the purple broccoli into thin stems with only the smallest end bits removed. Similarly, remove only the very ends from the asparagus spears.

Bring a pan of salted water to the boil and blanch each of the vegetables separately for 1 minute, quickly removing one kind from the water before adding the next. It is essential, especially with the broccoli, that you refresh the vegetables under very cold water before moving on to the next stage so they retain their colour. Take care also with the carrot leaves that they wilt but don't fall apart.

Next, gently heat almost all of the butter and garlic in a large pan, reserving a little butter for the mushrooms, adding a dash of Tabasco and most of the fresh chives or thyme leaves. Also add the reserved saffron and liquid and stir briskly with a small whisk. Finally add the lime juice, finely chopped chilli and salt and pepper to taste. Continue to whisk for a minute or so. Set aside.

When ready to serve, sauté the chanterelles in a separate pan with the remaining butter and the tamari if using, for a minute. Add these and the rest of the vegetables to the saffron butter, turning them over gently and folding in the remaining chives or thyme at the same time.

Lay the potatoes out on the plate as described and build the baby vegetables up into a pile on top. Pour any remaining saffron and herb butter all over and serve garnished with any remaining chives.

CHICKPEA CASSEROLE

WITH SPINACH

This is one of the best-sellers at Cranks. You can make it more interesting by serving a rich Greek yoghurt on the side, abundantly mixed with chopped coriander and finely minced garlic. This and the chilli bean casserole (see page 110) benefit from this kind of cold contrast. The casserole can be made in advance and in fact improves by being left overnight so that the flavours of the herbs and spices can develop. But in that case, only add the spinach when you have re-heated the casserole the next day.

SERVES
4 – 6

INGREDIENTS

- 500 g / 1 lb chickpeas, soaked overnight or for at least 2 hours
- 1.25 kg / 2½ lb onions, diced
- 100 ml / 4 fl oz olive oil
- 2–3 cloves garlic, finely chopped
- 2 tsp ground coriander
- 2 tsp turmeric
- 1 tsp ground cumin
- 1 scant tsp ground bay leaf

- 1 tbsp paprika
- 200 g / 7 oz potatoes, cut into 2.5 cm / 1 in chunks
- 250 g / 8 oz carrots, cut into 2.5 cm / 1 in chunks
- 1 small piece fresh chilli, very finely chopped
- 250 g / 8 oz fresh spinach, washed and with the stalks removed
- dash of Tabasco
- salt and freshly ground black pepper

METHOD

Cook the soaked chickpeas in a pan of simmering water for 1½–2 hours until they are tender. Do not add any salt at any point as this hinders the tenderizing process.

Meanwhile, fry the diced onion in the olive oil until transparent. Add the garlic and all the herbs and spices and continue to fry, adding some water just before the garlic browns. Simmer gently for 5 minutes or more or until all the water is absorbed and you are left with a thick sauce.

Add the potatoes, carrots and chilli and enough water to just cover and cover with a lid. Stir regularly, adding more water if necessary until the potatoes and carrots are just barely tender. Add the chickpeas and continue to cook for a further 10–15 minutes so that they can absorb all the flavours. At the last minute, stir in the spinach so that it just wilts. Add more salt and pepper as well as Tabasco to taste. Serve hot.

PUMPKIN AND WATERCRESS GNOCCHI
WITH GREEN AND PURPLE BASIL

These gnocchi are sunshine-coloured with bright green and purple streaks. The watercress and spring onion cut through the sweet, thick consistency of the pumpkin and bring a crisp, fresh element to the gnocchi. Use a brightly coloured pumpkin with flesh that is neither too tough nor too watery.

SERVES

6

INGREDIENTS

- 750 g/ 1½ lb pumpkin or other squash
- 100 g / 4 oz plain white flour, sifted
- 40 g / 1½ oz Parmesan cheese, grated
- 25 g / 1 oz watercress leaves, shredded
- 1 spring onion, finely sliced, green part included
- 15 g / ½ oz small green basil leaves
- 15 g / ½ oz small purple basil leaves
- salt and freshly ground black pepper

FOR THE SAUCE

- 150 ml / 6 fl oz olive oil
- 25 g / 1 oz watercress, large stalks removed, then roughly chopped
- 25 g / 1 oz Parmesan cheese, grated
- 1 clove garlic, very finely chopped
- salt and freshly ground black pepper

METHOD

Peel and cut the pumpkin into 3 cm / 1¼ in chunks and place in a heavy-based saucepan, just covered with water and seasoned with a little salt and pepper. Bring to the boil, then simmer for 6–7 minutes until tender. Drain well, mash with a fork or potato masher and add the sifted flour. Mix well until thoroughly incorporated, then add the Parmesan, shredded watercress, sliced spring onion and the whole green and purple basil leaves. Add salt and pepper to taste. Shape the mixture with your fingers – lightly dipped in flour – into elongated pieces the size of walnuts and set aside.

To make the sauce, mix the oil, chopped watercress, Parmesan, garlic and salt and pepper in a bowl and set aside.

Bring a large pan of salted water to the boil. Test one gnocchi first to make sure that it does not fall apart when cooking. If it does, add a little more flour. Drop in the gnocchi and poach for 2 minutes until cooked and no longer floury.

Place the drained gnocchi in a large flat bowl, pour the sauce all over and serve at once.

HOMITY PIE

Homity Pie has been on the menu at Cranks since its very early days and it is a favourite with many regular customers. It first appeared on the menu as individual pies, with the filling set in individual wholemeal pastry cases. These were much imitated and can still be seen on deli counters. It was then decided that the mix, filling and warming and old-fashioned as it was, should form the whole of the dish, so out went the wholemeal pastry – in perfect timing with the demise of the old wicker lampshades and the faded image of 1960s vegetarians.

By a happy coincidence, it now fits perfectly into the revival of a good old-fashioned British home cooking. You could easily add a layer of tomato sauce in the middle or a layer of cooked spinach, or both.

SERVES
6

INGREDIENTS

- 1 kg / 2 lb potatoes
- 50 g / 2 oz butter
- 200 ml / 8 fl oz sour cream
- 25 ml / 1 fl oz sunflower oil
- 1 garlic clove, crushed

- 100 g / 4 oz petit pois
- 100 g / 4 oz onion, diced
- 75 g / 3 oz mature Cheddar cheese, grated
- salt and freshly ground black pepper

METHOD

Preheat the oven to 190°C/375°F/gas 5.

Peel the potatoes and place them in a pan of cold salted water. Bring to the boil and cook for 30 minutes until the potatoes are soft. Drain and add the butter, cream, oil, garlic and seasoning. Mash thoroughly with a potato masher.

Meanwhile, bring a separate smaller pan of salted water to the boil and add the petits pois. Blanch for 3–4 minutes and drain. Add the petits pois and onions to the potato mixture. Mix well and transfer to a buttered ovenproof dish. Finally, top with the grated cheese and bake in the preheated oven for 25–30 minutes until golden brown.

VEGETABLE PAELLA

By using an array of strongly flavoured ingredients, such as the black olives and the sundried tomatoes, this vegetarian paëlla loses none of the intense taste of the original. It is made here with short-grain organic brown rice which adds body to the dish.

SERVES

6

INGREDIENTS

- 500 g / 1 lb short-grain organic brown rice
- 1 tbsp turmeric
- 2 heaped tbsp paprika
- 3 tbsp tamari
- 1 clove garlic, cut in half
- a few strands of saffron
- 1 bay leaf
- 100 ml / 4 fl oz olive oil
- 100 ml / 4 fl oz water
- 500 g / 1 lb courgettes, chopped into large dice

- 2 red peppers, cut into 5 cm / 2 in pieces
- 1 large red onion, chopped into large dice
- 2 corn on the cob, kernels removed
- dash of Tabasco
- 3 cloves garlic, crushed
- 75 g / 3 oz sundried tomatoes in oil, cut into strips
- 100 g / 4 oz Provençal black olives, left whole
- 25 g / 1 oz parsley, finely chopped
- handful of fresh basil
- salt and freshly ground black pepper

METHOD

Place the rice in a heavy-based pan and cover with one and add water according to packet directions. Add a little of the turmeric and paprika to the water as well as the tamari, the clove of garlic, the saffron and the bay leaf. Bring to the boil and immediately reduce to a gentle simmer for the next 45 minutes or until there is no water left in the pan and several holes have appeared on the surface. Though this is not necessary, I rinse the rice under cold water to remove any stickiness as it has to cook again and is much better when it stays light with the grains well separated.

Meanwhile, heat three-quarters of the olive oil and add the remaining paprika and turmeric together with the water and cook on a gentle heat until no graininess can be detected in the spices. Add more water if necessary and simmer until reduced to a thick and homogenous paste.

Heat the remaining olive oil and sauté first the courgettes for a minute or so and then briefly the red peppers. Sauté the red onion separately so that it remains firm and add the corn kernels. Sauté briefly, adding the Tabasco, crushed garlic and season. Mix all the vegetables together and cook for 3–4 minutes, adjusting the seasoning.

Add the vegetables and the cooked spice sauce to the rice. Finally, add the sundried tomatoes, black olives and the fresh herbs. Stir well over a high heat for 2–3 minutes and turn out onto a dish. Serve at once.

BLACK AND RED BEAN CASSEROLE

WITH LIME AND CORIANDER CREAM

This is really a delicious vegetarian chilli and seems to be a perennial favourite. You can make the beans as spicy as you like and add fresh coriander and fresh chilli as a garnish. Lime in the yoghurt or sour cream is refreshing and delicious. The guacamole is lighter and more mousse-like than usual due to the high-speed food processing. Serve the casserole with flour or corn tortillas and grated cheese or tortilla chips and sour cream or both.

SERVES

6

INGREDIENTS

- 250 g / 8 oz red kidney beans
- 250 g / 8 oz black kidney beans
- 100 ml / 4 fl oz olive oil
- 100 g / 4 oz onion, diced
- 3–4 cloves garlic, finely chopped
- 1 tbsp paprika
- 1 piece fresh chilli, finely chopped
- 75 g / 3 oz carrots, chopped into 1 cm / ½ in cubes
- tomato sauce (see page 100)
- 75 g / 3 oz sweetcorn, fresh off the cob or frozen
- dash of Tabasco
- 1 bunch fresh coriander, leaves only
- salt and freshly ground black pepper

FOR THE LIME AND CORIANDER CREAM

- 200 ml / 8 fl oz sour cream or yoghurt
- handful of fresh coriander, roughly chopped
- juice of half a lime

FOR THE GUACAMOLE

- 2 ripe Hass avocados
- 4 tbsp water
- 2 cloves garlic, crushed
- 2 tbsp olive oil
- 2–3 ripe tomatoes, deseeded and finely chopped
- salt and freshly ground black pepper

METHOD

Soak the kidney beans overnight, then drain and boil in plenty of water until tender. This may take 1–2 hours.

Heat the olive oil in a pan and sauté the onion until brown, adding the garlic about halfway through the cooking. Add the salt, pepper, paprika, fresh chilli and the carrots and continue to cook until they are *al dente* and the spices have turned into a thick homogenous paste. Add the drained, cooked kidney beans and then the tomato sauce and simmer until reduced. Stir in the sweetcorn and cook for a further few minutes.

Finally, adjust the seasoning with Tabasco, salt and pepper. Continue to simmer gently for 6–7 minutes, taking care that it does not dry out and, more importantly, that the sauce and vegetables form a cohesive whole with no trace of wateriness. Remove from heat and add the fresh coriander.

For the lime and coriander cream, mix the sour cream or yoghurt with the second quantity of coriander as well as the lime juice and salt to your own taste.

To make the guacamole, peel the avocados, remove the stones, cut into quarters and place in a food processor with the water and the crushed garlic and olive oil. Blend to a smooth purée. Transfer to a bowl and add the tomatoes. Grind black peppercorns over the surface and serve at once to avoid discoloration.

PEA AND ASPARAGUS RISOTTO

WITH BROAD BEANS

Frozen broad beans, especially the baby variety, are consistently good. If time is precious, fresh young peas are available ready-podded in the summer. Frozen petits pois are a good substitute, but they must be French.

SERVES

6

INGREDIENTS

- 1.5 litres / 3 pints light vegetable stock (see page 42)
- 50 g / 2 oz unsalted butter
- 1 tbsp olive oil
- 1 onion, very finely chopped
- 375 g / 13 oz young fresh peas, or frozen petit pois
- 375 g / 13 oz broad beans, fresh or frozen
- 2 cloves garlic, very finely chopped
- 275 g / 9 oz Vialone Nano rice
- 250 g / 8 oz asparagus
- 2 tbsp flat leaf parsley, chopped
- 75g / 3 oz Parmesan cheese, freshly grated
- salt and freshly ground black pepper

METHOD

Bring the stock to the boil and keep simmering gently for use throughout the cooking process.

Heat half the butter and the olive oil in a heavy-bottomed saucepan and sauté the onion until pale golden and soft. Mix in the peas and broad beans at this stage, if using fresh ones, as well as the chopped garlic. Cook over a low heat for 10 minutes, adding a few spoonfuls of stock during the cooking. Add the rice and sauté for 2 minutes until it goes partly translucent. Add about half the stock to the rice. Stir well and bring back to the boil. Simmer gently, stirring occasionally and adding the rest of the stock a little at a time, until the rice is *al dente*.

Meanwhile, bring a pan of salted water to the boil and blanch the trimmed asparagus for 1 minute.

Just before serving, add the parsley and remaining butter. Season with salt and pepper and at the last minute, add 4 tbsp of the Parmesan and the asparagus. Serve at once with the remaining cheese handed round separately.

NOTE

If using frozen peas and broad beans, blanch them first in plenty of salted water, refresh and add them in a few minutes before the rice is done.

AUBERGINE
AND FENNEL SAUTE

This is a rich combination of vegetables enhanced by the meltingly soft consistency of the aubergines. Serve with polenta, pasta or even potatoes and a mixed salad for a light and satisfying meal.

INGREDIENTS

- 150 ml / 6 fl oz olive oil
- 2–3 cloves garlic, crushed
- 2 bulbs fennel, cut into 3 cm / 1½ in chunks
- 500 g / 1 lb aubergine, cut into 3 cm / 1½ in chunks
- dash of Tabasco

- handful of basil leaves
- 500 g / 1 lb tomatoes, cut into quarters
- 75 g / 3 oz fresh Parmesan cheese, sliced into fine slivers
- salt and freshly ground black pepper

METHOD

Heat the olive oil gently and stir in the crushed garlic. Add the fennel and immediately turn up the heat and sauté for 5–6 minutes, stirring constantly. Add the aubergine, the Tabasco and half the basil and continue to sauté for 12–14 minutes, or until the aubergine is cooked. Add a little water during cooking to loosen the vegetables and the juices that will stick to the base. Then add the quartered tomatoes, season and sauté for a further minute so the tomato softens only slightly. Turn out onto a dish garnished with the remaining basil and shaved Parmesan.

VEGETABLE SAUTE

WITH POLENTA GNOCCHI

This is a simple meal with the soft and moist polenta poured on top of the vegetables and set briefly under a hot grill. Finely shredded Parmesan and a drizzling of olive oil are all that's needed to make it delicious.

SERVES
6

INGREDIENTS

- 125 ml / 5 fl oz olive oil
- 350 g / 12 oz red onions, cut into 4 or 6 pieces depending on size
- 2 cloves garlic, finely sliced
- dash of Tabasco
- 350 g / 12 oz fennel, cut into 5 cm / 2 in chunks
- 150 ml / 5 fl oz water
- 350 g / 12 oz aubergines, cut into 5 cm / 2 in chunks
- 350 g / 12 oz courgettes, cut into 2.5 cm / 1 in slices
- 1 red pepper, grilled, skinned and cut into 1 cm / ½ in wide strips (see page 173)

- 6 tomatoes, blanched, skinned, cut into quarters and deseeded
- several leaves of basil
- large handful of washed baby spinach
- salt and freshly ground black pepper

FOR THE TOPPING

- 350 g / 12 oz polenta
- salted boiling water
- 75 g / 3 oz Dolcelatte cheese (optional)
- 1 tbsp olive oil
- 75 g / 3 oz Parmesan cheese

METHOD

Heat the oil in a pan and add the chunks of red onion together with a little salt, pepper, garlic and a dash of Tabasco. Remove from heat before they discolour. Then, in the same pan, sauté the fennel, adding a little water and seasoning until gently brown but still firm. Remove, then add the chunks of aubergine and sauté so that they turn gold but retain their shape. Do the same with the courgettes.

Return all vegetables to the pan and add the red pepper and tomato and basil leaves. Toss over a high heat for 4–5 minutes. Remove from heat and add a large handful of spinach and toss until just wilted. Place the vegetables in an ovenproof dish or 6 individual dishes.

Prepare the polenta according to the method on page 88. Stir in the Dolcelatte if using, and pour the polenta over the vegetables. Lightly mark the top with a fork. Drizzle with olive oil and place under a hot grill for 2–3 minutes until just beginning to crisp. Sprinkle generously with freshly grated Parmesan and serve at once.

LAYERED GRILLED VEGETABLE RING

This elegant dish looks good on buffet tables. It can be made a day or so in advance, covered and refrigerated, but be sure to serve warm or at room temperature.

SERVES
6 - 8

INGREDIENTS

- 2 Mozzarella cheeses, cut into 8 slices each
- 125 ml / 5 fl oz olive oil
- 3 cloves garlic, crushed
- dash of Tabasco
- 1 large aubergine, cut into 5 mm / ¼ in slices
- 2 bulbs fennel, cut into 5 mm / ¼ in slices
- 3 medium courgettes, cut lengthways into thick slices
- 2 bunches spring onions, trimmed
- 2 red and 2 yellow peppers, grilled, peeled and cut into 6 (see page 173)

- 1 tbsp balsamic vinegar
- salt and freshly ground black pepper
- basil leaves, for garnish

FOR THE SAUCE
- 100 ml / 4 fl oz olive oil
- 100 g / 4 oz very red sundried tomato purée
- 4 tbsp warm water
- dash of Tabasco
- dash of balsamic vinegar
- a few small basil leaves

METHOD

Marinate the Mozzarella slices in a third of the olive oil with salt, pepper, Tabasco and some of the crushed garlic. Set aside.

Make the sauce by stirring the olive oil into the sundried tomato purée, then adding the warm water and the seasoning. Set aside.

Preheat the grill. Baste all the vegetables except the peppers with olive oil and sprinkle with salt, pepper and the crushed garlic. Lay the aubergine slices on a baking tray and grill on both sides until well browned. Repeat with the fennel, then the courgettes and the spring onions. Take care with the latter as they brown quickly.

Place all the vegetables in a bowl, add the balsamic vinegar and allow to cool.

Layer the vegetables inside a 25 cm / 10 in ring mould. Begin with the aubergine slices and follow with the sliced Mozzarella and the rest of the vegetables, completing with the courgettes and peppers laid in stripes on the final layer.

Place an upturned plate on top of the mould and turn so the plate is right-side up. Carefully remove the ring to reveal the many colours. Serve with the sauce and chunks of olive bread, green and black olives and garnish with loosely scattered basil leaves.

SUNDAY ROAST

WITH ROASTED VEGETABLES
AND MUSHROOM AND ONION SAUCE

A most traditional-looking roasted dinner and one we have served as the Cranks Christmas Special. If this doesn't seem like enough, you can also serve with Baby Brussels Sprouts (see page 154).

(see page 154).

SERVES
6

INGREDIENTS

- 50 ml / 2 fl oz olive oil
- 500 g / 1 lb onions, diced
- 3 cloves garlic, crushed
- 250 g / 8 oz ground almonds
- 250 g / 8 oz matzo meal
- 250 g / 8 oz carrots, shredded
- 1 tsp bouillon powder
- 1 heaped tbsp parsley, finely chopped
- 1 heaped tbsp fresh coriander, left whole
- pinch of nutmeg
- 2 eggs, size 3, beaten

FOR THE FILLING

- 50 ml / 2 fl oz olive oil
- 100 g / 4 oz onion, diced
- 250 g / 8 oz prunes, soaked in water
- 1 clove garlic, finely chopped
- 1 tsp bouillon powder
- salt and freshly ground black pepper

METHOD

Heat the oil and fry the onion and crushed garlic until pale gold in colour. Remove from heat and add all other ingredients. Mix thoroughly with a wooden spoon and set aside.

Meanwhile, make the filling. Heat the olive oil and fry the onion until brown. Add the soaked prunes and some of the water they have been soaking in. Simmer gently for about 10 minutes, adding the garlic and bouillon powder.

Preheat the oven to 200°C/400°F/gas 6. Oil a sheet of foil 30 x 30 cm / 12 x 12 in and place the ground almond mixture at one end, shaping it into a long sausage about 10 cm / 4 in in diameter and 30 cm / 12 in long. With your fingers, make a deep indentation that extends from one end to the other and place the prune filling into it. Then bring the almond mixture round to enclose the filling and press with your fingers to seal, smoothing with the palm of your hand as you go. Wrap tightly in the foil so that it does not dry out and place in an ovenproof dish half filled with boiling water. Bake in the oven for 35 minutes until set to the touch.

Serve 2 slices of the almond and prune roll per person, with a square of the potatoes, the roasted carrots and parsnips, the Brussels sprouts and the sauce.

INGREDIENTS

ROASTED PARSNIPS AND CARROTS

- 6 whole large carrots
- 6 whole large parsnips
- 50 ml / 2 fl oz olive oil
- 2 cloves garlic, crushed
- salt and freshly ground black pepper

METHOD

Peel and cut the carrots and parsnips into 4 even-sized batons. Mix with all other ingredients and place in an ovenproof dish in the oven and roast for 35 minutes until browned and tender.

INGREDIENTS

POTATOES

- 1.5 kg / 3 lb potatoes, finely sliced no more than 2.5 mm / ⅛ in thick
- 1 medium onion, very finely sliced
- 3 cloves garlic, crushed
- salt and freshly ground black pepper

METHOD

Mix the potatoes with the onion, garlic, salt and pepper and place in an ovenproof dish. Cover tightly with foil and bake in the preheated oven for 50 minutes until the potatoes are tender and golden brown on the bottom when turned out. Cut into neat squares for serving.

INGREDIENTS

FOR THE SAUCE

- 100 g / 4 oz onions, diced
- 50 ml / 2 fl oz olive oil
- 100 g / 4 oz field, chestnut or other dark mushrooms, roughly chopped
- 2 cloves garlic, finely crushed
- 50 ml / 2 fl oz red wine
- 1 heaped tsp cornflour
- salt and freshly ground black pepper

METHOD

Fry the onion in the olive oil until brown and add the roughly chopped mushrooms. Continue to sauté for a couple of minutes and add the garlic and red wine. Dissolve the cornflour in a little cold water and stir into the sauce. Bring back to the boil so that it just thickens.

NOTE

Set the oven at 200°C/400°F/gas 6 for all the vegetables.

FILLED FIELD MUSHROOMS
WITH PUY LENTILS

It is often a challenge to use ingredients whose colours and texture are reminiscent of the earth without ending up with dull and unappetizing dishes. Yet here is a dish which, whilst satisfying the appetite, is colourful and contemporary.

INGREDIENTS

SERVES
6

- 500 g / 1 lb Puy lentils
- 750 ml / 1½ pints water
- 1 sprig fresh basil
- juice of half a lime, plus half a lime to add to lentils
- 4 cloves garlic
- 6 large open cap mushrooms
- 5 tbsp olive oil
- 2–3 tbsp tamari
- dash of Tabasco

- 1 bulb fennel, chopped
- 1 tbsp brandy
- 1 red and 1 yellow pepper, grilled, peeled and cut into strips (see page 173)
- 1 tbsp balsamic vinegar
- 100 g / 4 oz baby spinach
- 1 handful fresh coriander, roughly chopped
- 150 ml / 6 fl oz yoghurt
- salt and freshly ground black pepper

METHOD

Place the lentils in a pan of cold water and bring to the boil. Do not add salt at this stage as this inhibits the cooking process but add a sprig of fresh basil, half a lime cut into quarters and two whole garlic cloves. Simmer gently for 35–40 minutes until the lentils are tender but still firm.

Meanwhile, remove the stalks from the mushrooms, chop and set aside. Sauté the whole mushroom caps for 5 minutes in 2 tbsp of olive oil, 1 tsp of tamari, a dash of Tabasco and a clove of crushed garlic. Remove from heat and reserve any juices that may be left in the pan.

Sauté the fennel in 1 tbsp of olive oil and half a clove crushed garlic and when tender, add the chopped mushroom stalks. Add the cooked lentils, reserved mushroom liquor, brandy and remaining tamari.

Sauté the pepper strips briefly in an almost dry frying pan with the balsamic vinegar, then add the spinach. Fold into the lentil mixture and fill each of the mushrooms generously.

Finally, add the scant juice of half a lime, the remaining crushed garlic, the coriander leaves and a little salt and pepper to the yoghurt and serve a spoonful of it with each mushroom.

BUTTERBEAN CASSEROLE WITH CIDER

The golden rules when cooking pulses are: do not undercook and do not overcook. A butterbean, a chickpea, a haricot bean or a flageolet must be soft and with no trace of a white, hard centre and yet should be whole and not reduced to soup. Pulses should not be salted during the cooking process – the salt prevents them from going soft – but once cooked, do not be mean with it. Make sure that when you cook pulses, they simmer slowly, with enough oil and sufficient spicing to render them rich, delicious and succulent. You can then indulge in some of the oldest known dishes, enjoying the chanas of India, the hariras of Morocco, the minestrones of Italy, the baked beans of America.

INGREDIENTS

- 500 g / 1 lb butterbeans
- 400 g / 14 oz onions, diced
- 3 cloves garlic
- 100 ml / 4 fl oz olive oil
- 250 g / 8 oz carrots, cut into 2.5 cm / 1 in chunks
- dash of tamari
- 100 ml / 4 fl oz cider
- 250 g / 8 oz courgettes, cut into 2.5 cm / 1 in chunks
- 150 g / 5 oz button mushrooms
- 250 g / 8 oz sweetcorn kernels, frozen or taken off the cob
- handful of fresh basil
- handful of fresh coriander
- salt and freshly ground black pepper

METHOD

Boil the butterbeans in plenty of water until they are tender but still intact.

Meanwhile, sauté the onion and garlic in the heated olive oil until pale gold in colour. Add the chunks of carrots and continue to sauté for a minute or two, adding a little tamari and some of the cider. Then add the courgettes and sauté for a further minute so that they don't lose their colour. Add the mushrooms, sauté for a few minutes, adding a little more tamari and a little more cider as well as salt and pepper to taste. Finally, add the sweetcorn and continue to stir. Add the cooked butterbeans with a little of the liquid they have cooked in and simmer gently for a further 10 minutes, adding the remaining cider so that all the flavours come together. Mix with plenty of freshly chopped basil and coriander and serve.

PAN-FRIED NOODLES

WITH SEARED TOFU, VEGETABLES
AND CASHEW NUTS

An Asian-inspired meal in a wok – the sizzling and searing
and the multitude of smells will make you want to eat a very
large bowl of this. Some touches, such as the grilled and
skinned peppers, are Mediterranean of course, as is the
addition of balsamic vinegar.

I have a cheap but lethal vegetable slicing machine made
to imitate a proper mandolin, with a julienne attachment to
cut all manner of vegetables into perfect matchsticks.
Without this, a mandolin or a similar attachment in a food
processor, you will have to cut the courgettes and carrots
into matchsticks by hand.

INGREDIENTS

SERVES

6

- 100 ml / 4 fl oz olive oil
- 2 tsp sesame oil
- 100 g / 4 oz carrots, cut into thin julienne strips
- 100 g / 4 oz courgettes, cut into thin julienne strips
- 1 red and 1 yellow pepper, chargrilled and peeled (see page 173), then cut into neat 5 mm / ¼ in strips with all the white pith removed
- 100 g / 4 oz mangetout
- 115 g / 4½ oz baby corn
- 100 g / 4 oz leeks, sliced finely on the slant
- 50 g / 2 oz aubergine, cut into thin julienne strips
- 1 tsp Tabasco
- 2 tbsp tamari
- 1 tbsp Ume Su

- 1 tbsp balsamic vinegar
- 1 tsp freshly grated ginger or galangal
- 2 cloves garlic, crushed
- ½ fiery red chilli, very finely sliced
- large handful of coriander leaves, picked off the stalks, half reserved for garnish
- 100 g / 4 oz smoked tofu, cut into thin strips
- 25 g / 1 oz cashew nuts
- 750 g / 1½ lb thick egg noodles, cooked
- 1 egg, beaten
- 4 tbsp sesame seeds
- 2 spring onions, sliced finely on the slant, reserved for garnish
- 1 heaped tbsp chives, neatly and finely chopped, reserved for garnish

METHOD

Heat a little of the olive and sesame oils in a wok and sauté the carrots for less than a minute so that they remain *al dente*. Remove from the heat and fry each of the vegetables in turn, seasoning with the Tabasco, tamari, Ume Su, balsamic vinegar, ginger, garlic, chilli and half of the coriander as you go. Regularly moisten the pan with water to loosen the juices which adhere to it but only add a drop of oil when absolutely necessary and only between vegetables. Sauté the tofu strips until gold and crisp and reserve some for garnish.

In an almost completely dry pan, toast the cashew nuts until they are golden brown and charred in places. Set aside.

Now return all the stir-fried ingredients and the noodles to the pan and continue to sauté for a couple of minutes.

Remove from the heat and stir in the beaten egg. Use a fork to twist a separate serving onto each plate and garnish liberally with toasted cashews, sesame seeds, spring onion, tofu strips, chives and coriander.

NOODLES

WITH PUMPKIN, COCONUT MILK, CORIANDER, LIME AND FRESH CHILLI

I cannot imagine that there was once a time when coriander was frowned upon, even sneered at, when coconut milk was as dimly known as the exotic and far-off land from which it hails, when limes were something you only saw in thin slices at cocktail parties and eating chilli a daredevil act for drunken men. Three cheers for culinary expansion – this dish is a triumph of flavours and easier to make than pie.

SERVES

6

INGREDIENTS

- 500 g / 1 lb pumpkin, cut into 2.5 cm / 1 in chunks
- 150 g / 6 oz carrots, cut into 2.5 cm / 1 in slices
- 100 ml / 4 fl oz sunflower oil
- 3 cloves garlic, crushed
- dash of Tabasco
- 150 g / 6 oz courgettes, cut into 2.5 cm / 1 in slices

- 100g / 4 oz onions, diced
- 750 g / 1½ lb Udon or egg noodles
- 250 ml / 10 fl oz coconut milk
- handful of fresh coriander
- ½ fresh chilli, sliced very finely
- salt and freshly ground black pepper

METHOD

Preheat the oven to 220°C/425°F/gas 7.

Place the pumpkin chunks, carrots and 2 tbsp of the oil in an ovenproof dish. Add a little crushed garlic, salt and pepper and a dash of Tabasco. Repeat with the courgettes in a separate dish as they will take slightly less time to cook. Place the pumpkin in the preheated oven and roast for 20–25 minutes until browned and tender. If there's room in your oven, roast the courgettes at the same time but check them after about 10 minutes and remove when browned. Alternatively, roast the courgettes after the pumpkin.

Meanwhile, fry the onion in the remaining oil until golden and set aside. Cook the noodles in plenty of salted boiling water, drain and set aside.

When the vegetables are cooked, add to the fried onion and pour in the coconut milk. Simmer gently for 2 minutes and add the fresh coriander and chilli, reserving some of each for garnishing. Add the noodles, stir and serve at once with a garnish of fresh coriander and chilli.

RATATOUILLE

This is my version of ratatouille made without tomatoes. In this recipe, the bright red comes from the vibrant colour of the best quality sweet paprika, slowly cooked in fragrant olive oil. The courgettes and peppers can stay quite firm.

SERVES
6

INGREDIENTS

- 100 ml / 4 fl oz olive oil
- 500 g / 1 lb (generous) aubergine, cut into 2.5–3 cm / 1–1¼ in chunks
- 250 ml / 10 fl oz water
- 1 tbsp paprika
- 4 cloves garlic, crushed
- dash of Tabasco
- 350 g / 12 oz courgettes, cut into 2.5 cm / 1 in slices
- 1 red pepper, ½ yellow pepper and ½ green pepper, each cut into 5 cm / 2 in neat squares
- salt and freshly ground black pepper

METHOD

Heat the olive oil in a large pan. Add the aubergine and sauté for 8–10 minutes, adding a little water if it begins to stick to the pan. Add the paprika, crushed garlic and Tabasco. Then add the courgettes and sauté until they begin to go soft and the aubergine dissolves in parts to form the basis of a sauce. Continue to simmer gently for 8–10 minutes, covering with a lid but stirring at regular intervals. Finally add the chunks of pepper and a little more water if necessary, continuing to sauté the vegetables for about 5–6 minutes over a high heat until the peppers have just begun to soften but retain their colour. The sauce should be thick and red from the paprika, so add water only to loosen the juices from the bottom of the pan and to make a paste with the slowly dissolving aubergine. Some of the aubergine must, however, remain intact.

Ratatouille is better when the flavours have been allowed to develop so you may wish to remove it from the heat, let it cool and heat it through again just before serving with large chunks of warm bread, a simple baked potato or small new potatoes tossed in olive oil.

FILLED PEPPERS

WITH YOGHURT AND CORIANDER SALSA

Filled peppers are delicious, especially if the peppers are roasted first and the filling is kept as fresh and crisp as possible. Tinned cannellini beans work well in this filling.

SERVES

6

INGREDIENTS

- 6 whole red peppers
- 3 cloves garlic, crushed
- 125 g / 5 oz red onions, diced
- 1 tbsp olive oil
- 500 g / 1 lb courgettes, diced into 1 cm / ½ in pieces
- 1 tsp grain mustard
- dash of Tabasco
- 320 g / 12 oz cannellini beans, cooked weight
- few leaves of fresh basil, chopped
- sprig of fresh coriander, chopped
- sprig of fresh parsley, chopped
- 25 g / 1 oz spring onion, chopped
- salt and freshly ground black pepper

FOR THE SALSA

- 250 ml / 10 fl oz plain or Greek yoghurt
- 5 tbsp water
- 2 spring onions, neatly and finely chopped
- handful of fresh coriander, chopped
- 1 clove garlic, crushed
- 1 tsp cumin (optional)

METHOD

Preheat the grill. Place the whole peppers on a baking tray with a very light sprinkling of salt and pepper and a crushed clove of garlic. Place under the hot grill, turning frequently so that the skins just begin to char all the way round. Allow to cool, then remove the tops, seeds and pith. Set aside.

To make the salsa, mix all the ingredients together and set aside.

Sauté the red onion for 1–2 minutes in the heated olive oil so that it retains its colour. Add the diced courgette, remaining crushed garlic, grain mustard and Tabasco and sauté for a further 5 minutes. Add the drained, cooked cannellini beans and stir carefully. Add the chopped herbs and the chopped spring onion. Fill each pepper generously, and serve with the salsa.

KUMARA PIE

Kumara is the Maori name for sweet potatoes and this is a dish that has found its way onto New Zealand menus. The layering effect is the same as for Gratin Dauphinois but there is no cheese and the potatoes crisp up and caramelize in their own sugars. I find the combination of sour cream and double cream works to rich perfection but it is equally possible with only one or the other. The garam masala and nutmeg are subtle additions which do not mask the sweetness of the potatoes.

SERVES

6

INGREDIENTS

- 1 kg / 2 lb sweet potatoes
- 25 g / 1 oz butter
- 100 g / 4 oz onions, very finely sliced into rings
- 500 ml / 1 pint sour cream
- 125 ml / 5 fl oz double cream
- 1 level tsp garam masala
- large pinch of nutmeg
- 1 clove garlic
- salt and freshly ground black pepper

METHOD

Preheat the oven to 180°C/350°F/gas 4.

Peel the potatoes, removing any black eyes. Cut into 5 mm / ¼ in thick slices. Rub the sides of an ovenproof dish with a little of the butter and cut the rest into small cubes. Mix all ingredients together and spread evenly into the dish. Place in the preheated oven and cook for at least 1 hour until the potatoes are soft and some are beginning to go crisp and brown on top.

Serve with a simple watercress salad, lightly dressed with a touch of lemon and a light olive oil.

BOSTON BAKED BEANS

Like my ratatouille on page 126, this is another example of a dish whose red hue owes everything to paprika and nothing at all to tomatoes.

Like my ratatouille on page 126

SERVES

8

INGREDIENTS

- 750 g / 1½ lb haricot beans (uncooked weight), soaked overnight
- 750 g / 1½ lb onions, diced
- 5 tbsp olive oil
- 1 heaped tbsp paprika
- 3 cloves garlic, crushed

- 750 ml / 1½ pints water
- 50 g / 2 oz molasses
- dash of Tabasco
- 10 vegetarian sausages, sliced
- 1 tbsp finely chopped parsley
- salt and freshly ground black pepper

METHOD

Place the haricot beans in a pan, cover with water and bring to the boil. Cook for about 1 hour until nearly tender, then drain.

Fry the onion until golden brown in two-thirds of the oil, then add two-thirds of the paprika and crushed garlic. Sauté for 4–5 minutes, then add the beans and the water. Bring back to a simmer. Cover with a lid and stir occasionally, cooking until the beans are soft which may take up to 1½ hours. You may complete this stage of the cooking in a pressure cooker which will take considerably less time (about 15–20 minutes). Add the molasses, Tabasco and salt and pepper to taste.

Meanwhile, heat the rest of the oil, add the remaining paprika and sauté the sausages until they are crisp and brown on both sides. Add to the beans and simmer for a further 7–8 minutes. Garnish with a little finely chopped parsley and serve.

savoury tarts

Crisp, golden pastry packed with innovative and mouth-wateringly good fillings – the savoury tarts in this chapter are light years away from the sad and sorry quiches found in the supermarket's chilled cabinet.

Few dishes have suffered the inequities of the quiche. I found it hard to use the word when writing this chapter as it so often refers to the sad imitations that still fill deli shelves and chilled cabinets. Instead, imagine light, crisp, melting pastry, made with butter and Parmesan and fresh herbs. Imagine a soft, rich, creamy filling using many different vegetables.

A successful tart needs to be made in a shallow loose-based tin that has been well floured and buttered. The pastry should be rolled out thinly, laid inside the tin, pressed against the sides and then pricked all over with a fork. Chill the pastry case for at least 30 minutes. Bake the case first until it is pale gold and crispy and allow it to cool slightly before adding the filling and baking again. If you use an egg-based filling, make sure that you bake it only until it is just set and light golden in colour.

CHERRY TOMATO TART

WITH FETA CHEESE AND BLACK OLIVES

A pretty summer tart, which is just as good hot or cold. It is best made in a fluted rectangular tin. The Feta cheese and black olives are both so salty that you will need no additional salt.

SERVES

6

INGREDIENTS

FOR THE PASTRY

- 150 g / 6 oz plain flour, sifted
- pinch of salt
- 75 g / 3 oz butter, diced
- 50 g / 2 oz Gruyère or Parmesan cheese, grated
- 1 egg yolk, size 3

FOR THE FILLING

- 250 g / 8 oz Feta cheese, crumbled
- 250 g / 8 oz black olives. stoned and chopped
- 2 heaped tbsp basil, roughly shredded, plus whole leaves for garnish
- 500 g / 1 lb cherry tomatoes

METHOD

To make the pastry, place the flour, salt and butter on a board or in a large bowl and rub lightly with your fingers until the mixture resemble fine breadcrumbs. Stir in the cheese. Mix the egg yolk with about 2 tbsp of very cold water and add to the flour. Bring together with a circular motion of your opened-out fingers and turn out onto a lightly floured board. Knead for 5–6 minutes until smooth, then wrap in cling film and refrigerate for about 20 minutes.

Meanwhile, mash the crumbled Feta cheese together with the chopped olives and add the shredded basil. Set aside.

Butter and flour a rectangular tin, 35 x 11 cm / 14 x 4½ in. Roll out the pastry onto a lightly floured surface. Line the tin with the pastry and prick all over with a fork. Set aside for 30 minutes, preferably in the fridge.

Preheat the oven to 200°C/400°F/gas 6. Bake the pastry case in the preheated oven for 10 minutes or until golden brown. Allow to cool slightly, then spread the Feta and olive mixture evenly all over the pastry base. Arrange the tomatoes on top and return to the oven for 15 minutes until the skins have burst and the tomatoes look slightly shrivelled in places. Garnish with the whole basil leaves before serving.

BROCCOLI AND DOLCELATTE TART
WITH MASCARPONE

The tart is loosely covered with baking parchment before baking which prevents the broccoli from going black. The Mascarpone combined with the Dolcelatte results in a more delicate tart than you might expect.

SERVES
8

INGREDIENTS

- prebaked pastry base (see page 135)
- 500 g / 1 lb broccoli
- 6 eggs, size 3
- 250 g / 8 oz Mascarpone cheese
- 150 g / 6 oz Dolcelatte cheese
- salt and freshly ground black pepper

METHOD

Preheat the oven to 220°C/425°F/gas 7. Separate the broccoli into florets and blanch in a pan of salted boiling water for 2 minutes. Drain well then arrange over the pastry base. Beat the eggs, Mascarpone and Dolcelatte together in a bowl with a hand-held mixer. Add salt and freshly ground black pepper and pour all over the broccoli and into the gaps. Cover loosely with baking parchment as mentioned above and bake for 20–25 minutes or until just set and serve.

NADINE'S PISSALADIERE

A traditional pissaladière from the south of France is usually made with a yeast dough and has anchovies on it. Because it is said to be a cross between a quiche and a pizza, I played around with it and came up with this version which could more properly be called a quichaladière. It is essential that the tomato sauce is very well reduced.

INGREDIENTS

FOR THE PASTRY

- 125 g / 5 oz butter, diced
- 100 g / 4 oz plain white flour, sifted
- 100 g / 4 oz plain wholemeal flour, sifted
- pinch of salt
- ice-cold water

FOR THE FILLING

- 1 large onion, peeled and sliced
- 50 ml / 2 fl oz olive oil

- 2 x 500 g / 1 lb tins whole, peeled tomatoes
- 3 cloves garlic, left whole
- pinch of brown sugar
- 50 g / 2 oz sundried tomatoes in oil, chopped
- handful of basil, left whole
- 350 g / 12 oz black olives, stoned and chopped
- 3 eggs, size 3
- 5 tbsp double cream
- 50 g / 2 oz Gruyère or smoked Cheddar, grated
- salt and freshly ground black pepper

METHOD

Make the pastry by rubbing the butter into the flours and salt until it resembles fine crumbs. Add the water and bring together to form a smooth dough. Wrap and refrigerate for 20 minutes.

Meanwhile, make the tomato sauce by frying the onion in the hot olive oil and adding the tinned tomatoes. Add the whole garlic cloves, sugar, sundried tomatoes and whole basil leaves. Cook for 40 minutes, stirring regularly until reduced to a thick consistency with no runny liquid. Retrieve the garlic and whole basil leaves and discard.

Preheat the oven to 220°C/425°F/gas 7. Butter and flour a 25 cm / 10 in loose-based tart tin, roll out the pastry and line the tin. Prick all over with a fork and bake in the preheated oven for 15 minutes until pale gold in colour.

Spread the chopped olives evenly over the pastry base and follow with a layer of tomato sauce. Beat the eggs, cream and cheese together and add a little salt and coarsely ground black pepper. Use a fork to make holes all over the olive and tomato layers (so that the custard can sink in) and pour over the egg mixture.

Return to the oven and bake for 15–20 minutes or until the top is gently set. A little runniness at this stage is acceptable as the custard will continue to set in its own heat once you have taken the tart out of the oven. Serve hot or warm.

MUSHROOM LATTICE TART

You could also make this as individual tartlets. A few wild mushrooms are all that's needed to create a deep and earthy flavour. Tamari, as usual, brings out the mushroom flavour perfectly and tarragon has long been associated with mushrooms, though if you find it too sweet, you could replace it with fresh thyme.

SERVES
8

INGREDIENTS

- double quantity pastry (see page 135), prebake the bottom and reserve half the dough for lattice top
- 25 g / 1 oz butter
- 1 kg / 2 lb button or chestnut mushrooms, sliced
- 100 g / 4 oz dried wild mushrooms, soaked in a little hot water to reconstitute and drained
- 3 cloves garlic, crushed
- large sprig fresh tarragon
- 1 tbsp tamari

- 1 tbsp brandy
- salt and freshly ground black pepper
- beaten egg, to glaze

FOR THE SAUCE
- 25 g / 1 oz butter
- 25 g / 1 oz flour
- 150 ml / 6 fl oz milk
- cooking liquor from the mushrooms

METHOD

Preheat the oven to 220°C/425°F/gas 7. Melt the butter in a saucepan over a low heat and add the mushrooms, the crushed garlic, tarragon, salt and pepper. Sauté for about 5 minutes. Add the tamari and the brandy and continue to sauté for a couple of minutes. Strain and reserve the liquor.

For the sauce, warm the milk until just before boiling point, melting the butter in another pan over a medium heat. Add the flour and stir thoroughly until completely amalgamated and the mixture comes away from the sides of the pan. Slowly pour the warm milk, stirring the whole time. Complete by adding the reserved mushroom liquor. Stir well and mix with the mushrooms.

Spread the mushroom mixture evenly over the pastry case and make the lattice by rolling out the remaining pastry and cutting out 14 strips each 1 cm / ½ in wide. Interweave them over the filling exactly as in the Dutch Apple Pie (see page 248). Lightly glaze the pastry with beaten egg and bake for 30 minutes until golden brown. Serve hot or warm.

GARLIC, OLIVE AND GRILLED COURGETTE TART

The boiled garlic gives this a pronounced, sweet garlic taste which is quite refined. Use a good full-looking head of garlic. A version of this tart was first made by Suzanne Cullen who now runs Culinary Arts for Cranks.

SERVES
8

INGREDIENTS

- prebaked pastry base (see page 135)
- 750 g / 1½ lb courgettes, sliced into 5 mm / ¼ in slices
- 25 ml / 1 fl oz olive oil
- dash of Tabasco
- 1 clove garlic, crushed

- 1–2 heads garlic, left whole
- 6 eggs, size 3
- 200 ml / 8 fl oz double cream
- 50 g / 2 oz green and black olives, stoned and roughly chopped
- salt and freshly ground black pepper

METHOD

Baste the courgette slices with olive oil, a little salt, Tabasco and the crushed garlic. Place under a hot grill and grill for 7 minutes on each side or until browned.

Preheat the oven to 220°C/425°F/gas 7. Meanwhile, bring a small pan of salted water to the boil and blanch the whole garlic for 7 minutes or until soft. Remove from the pan. Peel and scoop out the flesh.

Place the eggs, cream, peeled garlic, salt and pepper in a bowl and whisk briefly with a hand-held electric mixer. Stir in half the roughly chopped olives. Pour into the pre-baked pastry case and then arrange the courgettes and the remaining olives all over. Baked for 15–20 minutes or until set but still moist. Serve hot or warm.

FRENCH ONION TART

A classic and simple tart that remains one of the very best.
The onions need to be very well browned but must not go
black and adding a tablespoon of port or Marsala wine in
addition to the tamari makes the flavour richer and sweeter.
You might like to experiment using red onions.

INGREDIENTS

- prebaked pastry base (see page 135)
- 50 ml / 2 fl oz olive oil
- 1 kg / 2 lb onions, finely sliced
- 3 cloves garlic, crushed
- pinch of freshly ground nutmeg
- 1 tbsp Marsala wine

- 1 tbsp tamari
- 5 eggs, size 3
- 125 ml / 5 fl oz double cream
- 50 g / 2 oz Gruyère cheese, grated
- salt and freshly ground black pepper

METHOD

Heat the oil and gently fry the onion and garlic, seasoned with salt, freshly ground
black pepper and some freshly grated nutmeg for about 40 minutes or until a dark
golden brown. Raise the heat and add the Marsala wine and the tamari and fry for a
further 5 minutes, stirring all the time.

Preheat the oven to 220°C/425°F/gas 7. Spread the onion mixture evenly over the
pastry base. Beat the eggs with the double cream and add in the cheese and a little
more nutmeg and salt. Pour over the onion filling, making holes in the onion layer to
allow the egg mixture to seep through. Bake in the preheated oven for 20–25 minutes
or until set but still moist.

ROASTED BABY AUBERGINE TART

This must classify as one of the prettiest tarts of all and it is even prettier in a heart-shaped tin. Make it for a romantic meal and serve it with champagne, by candlelight.

SERVES
8 – 10

INGREDIENTS

- prebaked pastry base (see page 135)
- 500 g / 1 lb baby aubergines, cut in half
- 50 ml / 2 fl oz olive oil
- 3 cloves garlic, crushed
- dash of Tabasco
- 75g / 3 oz cherry tomatoes
- 50 g / 2 oz black olives, stones removed
- handful fresh basil, reserve the smallest leaves for garnish
- 4 eggs, size 5
- 200 ml / 8 fl oz double cream
- 50 g / 2 oz Parmesan cheese, freshly grated
- salt and freshly ground black pepper

METHOD

Baste the aubergine halves generously in the olive oil, crushed garlic and Tabasco and season with salt and pepper. Place under a very hot grill for 10 minutes, turning over at least once until the cut side is a dark golden colour and the skins are slightly charred.

Preheat the oven to 200°C/400°F/gas 6.

Arrange the aubergine halves all over the prebaked pastry base, cut side up. Fill the gaps with the cherry tomatoes, olives and basil. Mix the eggs, cream and Parmesan together and season. Pour all over, taking care to leave as much of the vegetables exposed as possible. Bake for 20–25 minutes or until set but still moist. Serve hot or warm.

GRILLED MEDITERRANEAN TART

The chunkiness of the vegetables and their vibrant colours, added to the fact that they are pre-roasted, gives this tart particular appeal. The eggs and cream act largely as a binder for the vegetables which should be abundantly in evidence.

INGREDIENTS

- prebaked pastry base (see page 135)
- 75 g / 3 oz red pepper, cut into 2.5 cm / 1 in squares
- 75 g / 3 oz fennel, cut into 4 cm / 1½ in chunks
- 75 g / 3 oz tomatoes, cut into quarters
- 75 g / 3 oz courgettes, cut into 1 cm / ½ in slices
- 5 tbsp olive oil
- 3–4 cloves garlic, crushed
- dash of Tabasco
- 4 eggs, size 5, beaten
- 200 ml / 8 fl oz double cream
- salt and freshly ground black pepper

METHOD

Preheat the oven to 240°C/475°F/gas 9.

Place the cut vegetables, olive oil, two-thirds of the crushed garlic, salt and pepper and a generous dash of Tabasco, in an ovenproof dish. Mix thoroughly, then bake in the preheated oven for 20 minutes or until charred and a little shrivelled in places.

Meanwhile, beat the eggs, cream and the remaining garlic together, season and set aside.

Reduce the oven temperature to 220°C/425°F/gas 7. Place the vegetables on top of the prebaked pastry base. Pour over the egg mixture and return to the oven for a further 20 minutes or until set. Serve hot or warm.

PUMPKIN TART

WITH WALNUTS, SPINACH AND PARMESAN

An unusual use of roasted pumpkin in a moist, delicate cream and egg base. The more you can stack up the pumpkin, the better.

INGREDIENTS

- prebaked pastry case (see page 135)
- 1.5 kg / 3 lb pumpkin, peeled and cut into 5 cm / 2 in pieces
- 2 tbsp olive oil
- 3 cloves garlic, crushed
- 250 g / 8 oz fresh spinach
- 50 g / 2 oz walnut pieces
- 250 ml / 10 fl oz double cream
- 6 eggs, size 3
- 50 g / 2 oz fresh Parmesan cheese, grated
- salt and freshly ground black pepper

METHOD

Preheat the oven to 230°C/450°F/gas 8.

Place the chunks of pumpkin in an ovenproof dish and baste with olive oil, salt, pepper and a little of the crushed garlic. Roast in the preheated oven for about 20 minutes or until browned on all sides.

Remove the pumpkin from the oven and reduce the heat to 180°C/350°F/gas 4. Add the spinach to the pumpkin and mix thoroughly until wilted in the heat. Then add the walnut pieces. Put the eggs in a bowl and beat well. Add the double cream, the remaining crushed garlic and salt and pepper. Finally, stack the pumpkin chunks and spinach in the pastry case. Pour the egg and cream mixture on top and in between the chunks but allow as much of the pumpkin to show through as possible. Bake for 20–25 minutes or until just set. Remove from oven whilst still moist and sprinkle with freshly grated Parmesan. Allow to cool for a few minutes, then eat immediately.

SWISS CHARD AND RADICCHIO TART

If, to your mind, radicchio has always been a salad leaf too bitter to use in anything but small quantities amidst a variety of more mild-mannered leaves, but you are nonetheless tempted by its unusual claret and burgundy colours, then you will be pleased with this recipe. Very gentle braising softens the flavours and provides a crisp contrast to the custard and the strong green of the chard. Garlic cooked in this way is gentler and less pungent than when used raw and adds a welcome sweetness to these components.

SERVES 8 – 10

INGREDIENTS

- prebaked pastry base (see page 135)
- 25 g / 1 oz butter
- 1 bunch Swiss chard, washed and chopped
- 1 large radicchio, washed and roughly torn
- 4 eggs, size 5
- 200 ml / 8 fl oz double cream
- 250 g / 8 oz cottage cheese
- 5–6 cloves garlic, blanched in boiling water until soft, then peeled and mashed
- salt and freshly ground black pepper

METHOD

Preheat the oven to 200°C/400°F/ gas 6.

Melt the butter and sauté the chard for a few minutes until wilted. Add salt and pepper and the radicchio and sauté for a further 1–2 minutes, so it is softened but retains its colour.

Mix the eggs, cream and cottage cheese together and add the mashed garlic. Arrange the roasted vegetables all over the pastry base and pour the egg mixture carefully on top, leaving as much of the vegetable exposed as possible. Bake for 20–25 minutes, or until set but still moist. Serve hot or warm.

vegetables &

side dishes

Inspired by world cuisines, this chapter celebrates the vegetable, from the humble cabbage enlivened with wild mushrooms, to Jerusalem artichokes roasted with red wine and Gruyère cheese and winter root vegetables baked in parchment parcels.

You will see by looking at the recipes that they can accompany some of the main course recipes to make an extra special meal. For everyday cooking, serve them with a simple rice or pasta dish to make a perfectly delicious meal in themselves. I hope that they will inspire you to create your own.

For more ideas, draw on the cooking of Asia, the Middle East and the Mediterranean countries – regions with a long, rich history of vegetarian cooking. Go to your nearest large supermarket, look carefully into Greek and Pakistani shops and examine the stalls in your local fruit and veg market. Ask about the exotic-looking, sculptural things you will see there. Learn their names and how to prepare and cook them. And most importantly of all, experiment.

ROASTED BABY SQUASH

SERVED WITH GREEK YOGHURT

Really, half a squash roasted in its own protective skin, soft as a purée, is a meal in itself. And the spoonful of Greek yoghurt is a cold luxury in between hot, sweet, garlicky mouthfuls.

SERVES

6

INGREDIENTS

- 3 squash, each approximately. 1 kg / 2 lb in weight
- 150 ml / 6 fl oz olive oil
- 1 tbsp tamari
- 12 cloves garlic, unpeeled
- 6 tbsp Greek yoghurt
- handful of fresh coriander leaves
- salt and freshly ground black pepper

METHOD

Preheat the oven to 200°C/400°F/gas 6.

Cut each squash in half and remove the seeds. Make diagonal cuts into the flesh but not all the way to the skin. Baste with the olive oil and tamari on both sides and season. Fill each half with the unpeeled garlic cloves and turn upside down onto an oiled ovenproof dish. Bake in the preheated oven for about 40 minutes or until the flesh feels tender when poked with a fork.

Remove from oven. Scoop out the flesh and place in a serving dish and mash roughly. Break open the garlic cloves and put them back into the squash and mash. Serve with a thick dollop of Greek yoghurt, spiked with several coriander leaves. Lightly sautéed green beans (or mangetout, broccoli or asparagus) are all you will need on the side.

MANGETOUT, BABY CORN AND ASPARAGUS
WITH TOASTED SEEDS AND HIZIKI SEAWEED

This is a rapid vegetable stir-fry that can be served hot, cold and anything in between. Serve it with Camargue red rice mixed with wild rice and, if you like seaweed, add a tablespoon of Nori flakes to the rice before serving. If not, finely chopped fresh chives and roughly chopped fresh coriander will add colour and interest. Ume-Su is a Japanese vinegar made from pickled Umeboshi plums. It has a distinctive taste and is stocked by Japanese and wholefood stores.

SERVES
6

INGREDIENTS

- 2 heaped tbsp pumpkin seeds
- 1 heaped tbsp sesame seeds
- 100 g / 4 oz young asparagus, trimmed
- 1 tbsp olive oil
- 250 g / 8 oz baby corn
- 100 g / 4 oz mangetout, topped and tailed
- 2 tbsp water
- 1–2 tsp tamari

- 1–2 tsp Ume-Su
- 1 piece fresh chilli, 2.5 cm / 1 in long, finely chopped
- large handful of Hiziki seaweed, soaked in hot water and 2 tbsp tamari until tender, then drain
- salt

METHOD

Toast the seeds in a dry pan with some salt until they begin to pop and go golden brown. Set aside.

Bring a small pan of salted water to the boil (a milk pan is large enough). Immerse the asparagus and boil for precisely 1 minute. Drain and set aside.

Heat the olive oil in a large frying pan or wok. Add the baby corn and sauté for 3–4 minutes, tossing and turning all the time until they begin to wilt very slightly and to turn golden in places. Add the asparagus and continue to sauté for 30 seconds, then add the mangetout and sauté for a further minute or so. Tossing the pan about, quickly add the water which will sizzle in the heat, the tamari and Ume-Su. Finally add the finely chopped chilli and the drained and by now tender seaweed. Remove from heat and add the toasted seeds. Serve hot or cold.

BABY BRUSSELS

WITH PARMESAN AND NEW POTATOES

Brussels sprouts are as much a part of Christmas as tinsel
and carols and though you may belong to the breed that
exclaims in despair, "I hate Brussels sprouts, but it's
Christmas, we have to have Brussels sprouts," at the very
least try this method. Brussels sprouts are one of very few
vegetables I will still subject to boiling but, as you can see
from the recipe, only briefly. Don't waste precious time on
the older variety, but search instead for small young sprouts.
A generous knob of butter, some crushed garlic, lots of
Parmesan – this is an easy and quick resurrection which may
keep Brussels sprouts on your Christmas menu for years to
come.

INGREDIENTS

SERVES
6

- 500 g / 1 lb smallest new potatoes (olive potatoes)
- 500 g / 1 lb baby Brussels sprouts
- 25 g / 1 oz butter

- 1 clove garlic, crushed
- 25 g / 1 oz finely chopped parsley
- 50 g / 2 oz Parmesan cheese
- salt and freshly ground black pepper

METHOD

Place the potatoes in a pan of cold salted water and bring to the boil. Ten minutes into
the cooking time add the trimmed and cleaned Brussels sprouts and continue to boil
for another 3–4 minutes. Remove from heat and refresh under cold water.

Melt the butter in a saucepan and return the vegetables to the heat for 3–4 minutes,
together with the garlic and salt and pepper. Remove from heat and add the chopped
parsley. Turn out into a dish and garnish generously with fine shavings of Parmesan and
freshly ground black pepper.

SPLIT ROASTED POTATOES

There are times when it is best to leave classics and favourite dishes well alone and you may consider roast potatoes to be one such instance. Slicing them in this fashion however, quite apart from looking pretty, adds to their crispiness because it increases the surface area exposed to the sizzling oil.

SERVES
6

INGREDIENTS

- 1 kg / 2 lb roasting potatoes
- 100 ml / 4 fl oz olive oil

- 1 sprig fresh rosemary, leaves stripped
- salt and freshly ground black pepper

METHOD

Preheat the oven to its highest setting.

Peel the potatoes and keep in cold water while you work. Make parallel slits into the potatoes, taking care not to cut all the way through to the bottom. Sprinkle with salt and pepper and place in an ovenproof dish with the oil and the fresh rosemary, basting the potatoes generously. Then bake for 1 hour, turning occasionally so that the potatoes are crisp and golden on all sides.

BAKED VEGETABLES IN PARCHMENT

This is an unusual way of serving root vegetables with their sweetness gently brought out. Opening the bags to reveal the different vegetables is a real treat and especially pretty because the beetroot weeps some of its vermilion juices over the other vegetables.

SERVES
6 – 8

INGREDIENTS

- 250 g / 8 oz celeriac
- 250 g / 8 oz carrots
- 250 g / 8 oz beetroot
- 250 g / 8 oz Jerusalem artichokes
- 250 g / 8 oz sweet potatoes
- 250 g / 8 oz parsnips
- 250 g / 8 oz new potatoes
- 250 g / 8 oz baby onions, peeled
- 12 cloves garlic, unpeeled
- 50 ml / 2 fl oz olive oil

- 1 tbsp white wine
- 1 tbsp tamari
- salt and freshly ground black pepper
- 6–8 sheets of baking parchment 20 x 20 cm / 8 x 8 in wide

TO SERVE

- 250 g / 8 oz quark
- 3 cloves garlic, crushed
- handful of basil or other herb, finely chopped

METHOD

Preheat the oven to 190°C/375°F/gas 5.

Scrub all the vegetables clean and cut all but the potatoes and the baby onions into 3 cm / 1¼ in cubes. Mix the cut vegetables, potatoes, onions and garlic with the olive oil, white wine, tamari and salt and pepper.

Divide the vegetables equally between the sheets of baking parchment, wrap around, folding the edges tightly together to form a bag and place closely together on a baking tray. Place in the preheated oven for 35–40 minutes. Serve the vegetables in their packets, straight from the oven, with a bowl of quark, richly seasoned with crushed garlic, salt and pepper and herbs and let people spoon some over their vegetables as needed.

BRAISED CABBAGE

WITH WILD MUSHROOMS

Can it be true? Boring old cabbage in the same mouthful as wild mushrooms? Yes, if you braise the cabbage first, use double cream and give it a kick with grain mustard. You will actually taste it for the delicious vegetable it really is. Don't worry about it being soft – soggy is the only condition you have to avoid. The commonest of white cabbages will do, though a Savoy is a brighter, finer thing and requires a little less cooking time.

Serve this with creamed potatoes on a cold winter's day and go for a long walk afterwards.

SERVES

6

INGREDIENTS

- 1.5 kg / 3 lb white cabbage
- 1 tsp bouillon powder mixed into 100 ml / 4 fl oz hot water
- 65 ml / 2½ fl oz olive oil
- 3 cloves garlic, finely sliced
- 100 ml / 4 fl oz double cream
- 1 tsp grain mustard

- handful of chives, finely sliced
- 350 g / 12 oz chanterelle mushrooms
- 25 g / 1 oz butter
- a few leaves of fresh tarragon
- 1 tbsp tamari
- 1 tbsp red wine or brandy
- salt and freshly ground black pepper

METHOD

Trim the cabbage and remove the outer leaves. Chop it roughly and place in a heavy-based saucepan with the dissolved bouillon powder, oil, two finely sliced garlic cloves, salt and pepper. Cover with a lid and bring to the boil. Immediately lower the heat and braise gently for 20 minutes or until the cabbage is soft and tender and the liquid reduced by two-thirds. Add two-thirds of the cream and the mustard. Continue to simmer for just a few minutes, then remove from the heat and add almost all of the chives.

Meanwhile, carefully clean the mushrooms. Melt the butter in a pan and sauté them for just 2–3 minutes with the remaining garlic, a little salt and pepper and the tarragon. Add the remaining cream, the tamari and the wine or brandy. Bring to a gentle bubble and immediately remove from the heat. Place the hot cabbage in a warmed dish and pour the mushrooms and sauce over, garnishing with the remaining chives.

ROASTED JERUSALEM ARTICHOKES

WITH RED WINE

Despite their knobbly and earthy appearance, Jerusalem artichokes can have a sweet and delicate flavour, especially when cooked slowly as in this gratin. They are also delicious in soups with lemon and saffron. In this recipe, you don't even need to peel them – simply remove the coarser, knobbly bits. When preparing them, place them first in a bowl of cold water that has been acidulated with lemon to avoid discoloration. In this recipe, they absorb the red wine, tamari and olive oil juices and become even richer and more succulent.

INGREDIENTS

SERVES
6

- 600 g / 1¼ lb Jerusalem artichokes, cut in half
- 50 ml / 2 fl oz red wine
- 2 tbsp olive oil
- 1 tbsp tamari
- 2 cloves garlic

- dash of Tabasco
- handful of chives, finely chopped
- 100 g / 4 oz Gruyère cheese, grated (optional)
- salt and freshly ground black pepper

METHOD

Preheat the oven to 200°C/400°F/gas 6.

Mix all ingredients except the chives together and place in an ovenproof dish. Place in the preheated oven for 1 hour 10 minutes until the artichoke skins are withered, the flesh tender and succulent, and the juices have formed a rich and sticky sauce. Add the Gruyère if using, so that it melts in the heat of the artichokes and leaves a thread when lifted. Garnish with chives and serve with a mix of brown and wild rice, sautéed green beans and asparagus, and a green salad.

PUMPKIN AND MANGETOUT

WITH SEAWEED

Three such pronounced colours can only make this dish exciting to look at and what appeals to the eyes does not fail to whet the appetite. This is another simple vegetable combination that is as healthy and nourishing as you could wish. Serve this with simply prepared lemon rice and one other grilled or roasted vegetable dish. Butternut or acorn squash also works well in this recipe.

INGREDIENTS

- handful of Hiziki seaweed
- about 4 tbsp tamari
- 3 cloves garlic, crushed
- dash of Tabasco
- 100 ml / 4 fl oz light olive oil
- 900 g / 1¾ lb pumpkin, peeled and cut into 3 cm / 1 ¼ in chunks

- 1 piece ginger 3 cm / 1½ in, peeled and finely minced
- 150 g / 6 oz mangetout, topped and tailed
- small handful of fresh coriander leaves
- 1 piece fresh coconut
- 1 piece chilli, very finely chopped

METHOD

Place the seaweed in a bowl with half the tamari, a little of the garlic and a few drops of Tabasco. Cover with hot water and set aside until soft. Heat all but 1 tbsp of the oil gently, and add the pumpkin. Stir-fry for 3–4 minutes with most of the garlic and ginger, and Tabasco, turning over constantly with a wooden spoon until the chunks begin to soften on the outside and to mingle with the seasonings. Then add 2 tbsp of the tamari, a little at a time, taking care that it does not stick and burn. Add a little water if necessary.

Heat the remaining 1 tbsp oil in a separate pan and very quickly sauté the mangetout with 1 tsp tamari, and the remaining garlic and ginger, letting them stay as green as possible. Add to the pumpkin. Drain the seaweed and add, along with most of the coriander. Place on a large plate and using a metal cheese slicer, very finely slice the coconut so that it falls over the vegetables like a mass of petals. Garnish with the remaining coriander and chilli and serve immediately.

MIXED SQUASHES SAUTEED

WITH A FRESH HERB, GINGER AND LIME GLAZE

This dish is probably best made when you have a large crowd to feed, so that you can make the most of the many kinds of squash now available in most supermarkets. Cutting the squashes into pieces makes them much easier to peel.

SERVES
6 – 8

INGREDIENTS

- 1 acorn squash
- 1 butternut squash
- 500 g / 1 lb pumpkin
- 300 g / 10 oz patty pan squash
- 50 ml / 2 fl oz olive oil
- 50 g / 2 oz butter

- 1 heaped tsp ground ginger
- zest and juice of 1 lime
- 1 tbsp brown sugar
- dash of Tabasco
- sprig of fresh sage

METHOD

Cut the acorn squash, butternut squash and pumpkin into manageable segments, removing the seeds and peel. Cut all the squashes into 2.5 cm / 1 in chunks. Bring a large pan of salted water to the boil. Add the squashes and simmer gentle for 5–10 minutes, or until tender.

Meanwhile, place the olive oil and butter in a large pan and heat gently until the butter melts. Add the ground ginger, lime juice and sugar and cook for 2 minutes until the sugar has completely dissolved. Add the Tabasco, sage and lime zest, stir for 30 seconds and then add the squash. Heat through and serve at once with couscous and a green salad.

TEMPURA GREEN BEANS

These are perfect either as a starter or served at a drinks party. The trick is to fry these at the last moment to keep the batter light and crisp. Part of the water in the batter can be replaced by very cold lager which gives a more interesting flavour.

INGREDIENTS

- 1 litre / 2 pints sunflower oil
- 500 g / 1 lb green beans, topped, tailed and blanched for 1 minute
- salt

FOR THE BATTER

- 1 large egg, separated
- 350 ml / 12 fl oz very cold water
- 100 g / 4 oz plain flour
- pinch of salt

FOR THE DIPPING SAUCE

- 5 tbsp tamari
- 50 ml / 2 fl oz Ume-Su (see page 152)
- 25 g / 1 oz pickled daikon or pickled ginger, cut into fine strips
- dash of Tabasco

METHOD

Line a plate with several layers of kitchen paper. To make the dipping sauce, mix all the ingredients together and set aside.

To make the batter, mix the yolk with the cold water, sift the flour and salt into it and mix lightly. Then lightly whisk the egg white and add just one half of it to the mixture. Discard the rest.

Heat the oil until it is very hot and then turn the heat down. Immerse a few green beans at a time into the batter and then drop them carefully into the hot oil. As soon as they crisp up and rise to the surface (less than a minute), remove them with two forks or a pair of tongs, place them on the kitchen paper and sprinkle with salt while they are still very hot. Continue until all the green beans are fried.

Serve the green beans immediately, with the sauce in small bowls or ramekins so people can dip the beans themselves.

THREE BEAN AND VEGETABLE PUREES

These vegetable purées are extremely versatile. They are excellent as spreads in sandwiches and on toasts. They're also incredibly easy to make and several kinds on a buffet table look and taste great. The secret is in the olive oil, which should be extra virgin if possible, and in all the bits and pieces you add to them.

I used to shell the broad beans until I tested the recipe for this book and discovered that blending them longer removed this chore. The final result is still as bright and soft as spring leaves.

SERVES
6

INGREDIENTS

FOR THE BROAD BEAN PUREE
- 500 g / I lb broad beans, fresh or frozen
- 50 ml / 2 fl oz extra virgin olive oil, plus I tbsp for garnish
- 2 cloves garlic, crushed
- ½ tsp ground cumin
- I spring onion, very finely sliced
- salt and freshly ground black pepper

FOR THE CANNELLINI BEAN PUREE
- 400 g / 14 oz tin cannellini beans
- I tbsp olive oil
- 50 g / 2 oz sundried tomatoes in oil, thinly sliced
- 50 g / 2 oz black olives, pitted and roughly chopped
- few basil leaves
- salt and freshly ground black pepper

FOR THE ROOT VEGETABLE PUREE
- 500 ml / I pint light vegetable stock
- 25 g / I oz butter
- 350 g / 12 oz carrots, peeled and cut into I cm / ½ in chunks
- 350 g / 12 oz parsnips, peeled and cut into I cm / ½ in chunks
- 350 g / 12 oz celeriac or swede, peeled and cut into I cm / ½ in chunks
- salt and freshly ground black pepper
- 3 tbsp chopped parsley or coriander

METHOD

To make the broad bean purée, bring a pan of salted water to the boil and boil the beans for 5–6 minutes or until tender. Place in a food processor on its highest speed and blend for 8–10 minutes until absolutely smooth, slowly adding the olive oil, crushed garlic, salt and pepper and cumin as you do so. Transfer to a shallow bowl, pour the 1 tbsp olive oil on top and garnish with the finely sliced spring onion.

To make the cannellini bean purée, drain the beans and place in a food processor. Blend at high speed for a few seconds, adding the olive oil and salt and pepper at the same time. Transfer to a shallow bowl and fold in the slivers of sundried tomatoes and the olives. Garnish with the basil leaves.

To make the root vegetable purée, heat the stock until just boiling and set aside. Melt the butter in a heavy-based saucepan and add the vegetables all in one go. Stir regularly for 5 minutes and add the hot stock. Bring back to the boil and simmer gently for 25 minutes, covered with a lid.

Check regularly that the vegetables are not sticking to the bottom of the pan and add a little more stock or water if necessary. Should there be any stock left by the time the vegetables are tender, strain it and drink as it is or reserve for a soup. Place the vegetables in a food processor and blend as smooth or as coarse as you like. Serve with a knob of butter and the chopped parsley or coriander.

GRILLED SHIITAKE MUSHROOMS
WITH SPRING ONIONS

Funny how something you might describe as chewy and slippery can turn out to be so delicious. Shiitake mushrooms, Japanese par excellence, yet commercially available thanks to the cultivating prowess of the Dutch, are delicious in all manner of Oriental dishes. They require just the briefest application of heat – a couple of minutes at most under a hot grill is all that is needed here. With an equally brief grilling of spring onions, this is a quick and sophisticated accompaniment. I like this served Oriental style, with several other vegetable dishes, each in its own bowl, each seasoned with individuality.

INGREDIENTS

- 750 g / 1½ lb shiitake mushrooms
- 5 tbsp olive oil
- 1 tbsp teriyaki sauce
- small piece fresh chilli, very finely chopped
- 2 cloves garlic, finely chopped
- 12 spring onions

- 5 tbsp water
- 3 tbsp peanut butter
- dash of Tabasco
- handful of fresh coriander, some reserved for garnish

METHOD

Simply remove the toughest bits of the stalk from the mushrooms. Mix the olive oil, teriyaki sauce, most of the chilli and garlic together into a sauce and brush the mushrooms with the sauce. Trim the spring onions of their hairy tails and baste with the same sauce. Place under a hot grill for a couple of minutes, turning over at least once until charred and softened.

Add the water to the peanut butter and stir to dissolve, adding the remaining garlic, chilli, Tabasco and coriander. Warm gently and serve with the mushrooms and spring onions, garnished with coriander leaves.

ROASTED WINTER VEGETABLES

These roasted winter vegetables are substantial enough to form the main part of a meal and are so easy to prepare that I have sometimes placed them in the oven, gone shopping and returned to a ready meal. Cubes of marinated plain or smoked tofu can be separately roasted for 20 minutes and added to the vegetables. Some of the vegetables will cook faster than others. The mushrooms, for instance will become quite shrivelled, but as long as they don't burn you will find this simply intensifies their flavour. Various sauces can also be served. See the tikka sauce with the chickpea fritters (page 78), with or without the addition of yoghurt, or a simple crème fraîche or fromage frais, seasoned with lemon or lime and any herb you fancy. You could also add a couple of spoonfuls of wine or brandy to the roasting vegetables and make them quite grand. A few slivers of wild or cultivated mushrooms can also greatly enhance the flavour.

SERVES
4 – 6

INGREDIENTS

- 4 medium carrots, peeled and cut into 1.5 cm / ¾ in chunks
- 4 medium parsnips, peeled and cut into 1.5 cm / ¾ in chunks
- 250 g / 8 oz shallots or baby onions, peeled and left whole
- 6 garlic cloves, unpeeled
- 3 medium potatoes, peeled or unpeeled and cut into wedges
- 4 leeks, trimmed and cut into 5 cm / 2 in lengths

- 500 g / 1 lb pumpkin, cut into 3 cm / 1¼ in chunks
- 150 g / 6 oz mushrooms
- 4 tbsp olive oil
- 1 tbsp mixed chopped herbs, such as thyme, rosemary and parsley
- 1 tbsp tamari
- pinch of soft brown sugar
- salt and freshly ground black pepper

METHOD

Preheat the oven to its highest setting. Mix all the vegetables together with the oil, herbs, tamari, sugar and salt and pepper and place in a large ovenproof dish or oven tray. Place in the oven and roast for 35–40 minutes or until all the vegetables are tender.

salads

Cranks has always maintained a reputation for its salads — huge bowls of fresh and colourful raw ingredients with interesting dressings and toppings. There is such an abundance of weird and wonderful produce available in shops and markets that the art of salad making is more interesting and exciting than ever.

Salads succeed best when served as a course in their own right. They can be composed of cooked ingredients and eaten warm, or dressed with an infinite variety of croûtons and seeds, slithers of dried fruit, or parings of strong cheese. Try them served with nothing but extra virgin olive oil and vinegar or dressed extravagantly with thick luxuriant sauces, creamy with blue cheese or biting with garlic and chilli. Nuts may be toasted and tossed in. Harder vegetables can be grated and left to marinate in thick, rich dressings, while delicate leaves require the thinnest of coatings just before serving.

SALADE CUITE (CHOUCHOUKA)

I have eaten my mother's salade cuite all my life and this is what we have always called it. It was only in writing the recipe for this book that my father recalled that it is in fact the Chouchouka of Algerian origin. The original is cooked slowly and for a long time and turned almost into a confit. I cook this recipe for far less time, which gives a much lighter result, but try it out both ways. In either case, do not skimp on the garlic.

INGREDIENTS

- I red, I green and I yellow pepper
- 50 ml / 2 fl oz olive oil
- 500 g / I lb ripe tomatoes, cut into quarters
- dash of Tabasco or cayenne pepper
- 5 cloves garlic, chopped

METHOD

Put the peppers under a hot grill until the skins are charred, turning at least once to char evenly. Put in a bowl and cover with a plate until cool enough to handle (this makes them easier to peel). Peel, deseed and cut into strips when they are cool enough to handle.

Heat the oil in a frying pan and add the chopped tomatoes. Fry for 4–5 minutes until broken down into a sauce. Add the Tabasco or cayenne pepper and the chopped garlic. Fry for a further 2–3 minutes, stirring regularly, then add the pepper strips and continue to cook for 3–4 minutes or, for a more authentic result, 10–12 minutes so that practically all the juice is evaporated and you are left with a thick sauce. Eat at room temperature as part of an antipasto, served with several other simple salads and chunks of warm bread of any nationality.

FENNEL AND TOMATO SALAD

This is a refreshing and clean-tasting salad. The fennel handles the much stronger flavours of garlic and olives surprisingly well. This salad works equally well served straightaway, or you can leave to marinate for an hour or so.

INGREDIENTS

- 6 small, perfect young fennel bulbs
- 3 cloves garlic, sliced paper thin
- 4 tbsp olive oil
- 2 tbsp balsamic vinegar
- 500 g / 1 lb ripe plum tomatoes
- 100 g / 4 oz Provençal black olives
- 50 g / 2 oz fresh Parmesan, cut into thin slivers
- salt and freshly ground black pepper

METHOD

Trim the fronds and ends from the fennel stalks. Slice thinly along the vertical grain. Either leave as is or cut the slices into thin strips. Mix the finely sliced garlic, oil, vinegar and salt and pepper and pour over the fennel. Allow to marinate for 20 minutes or so. Then add the tomatoes cut into wedges and finally the black olives and the Parmesan.

ROAST FENNEL, CHICORY AND ARTICHOKE SALAD

WITH FRESH GARLIC, PINE NUTS
AND SUNDRIED TOMATO DRESSING

There are sweet and bitter sweet flavours in this roasted and grilled vegetable salad and the younger and fresher the vegetables the better. Bunches of coriander can be kept in the fridge with their stems immersed in water.

INGREDIENTS

- 4 small, young bulbs fennel
- 3 heads chicory, red or white
- 2 x 135 g / 4½ oz tins artichoke hearts, cut in half, or 12 baby artichokes, hearts and stems only
- 2 bulbs fresh garlic, outer skin removed and each cut into 6
- 4–5 tbsp olive oil
- 1 tbsp very red sundried tomato purée
- 100 g / 4 oz herbed green olives
- 1 tbsp pine nuts, toasted
- bunch of coriander, chopped
- sea salt and freshly ground black pepper

METHOD

Preheat the oven to 240°C/475°F/gas 9. Trim the fennel and cut lengthways into 6 pieces. Trim the chicory, removing any old leaves, and cut into 6. Cut the artichoke hearts in half.

Mix the vegetables together with the garlic, olive oil and some sea salt and freshly ground black pepper. Place in an ovenproof dish. Bake in the preheated oven for 15 minutes and then place under a hot grill for 5–6 minutes to brown.

Remove from the heat, stir well and transfer to a large colourful plate. Just before serving, dot the sundried tomato purée all over, as well as the green olives and the toasted pine nuts and fresh coriander and mix. Serve warm or at room temperature.

PANZANELLA

This traditional Tuscan salad makes use of stale bread. Any crusty white bread will do, though if you have some, an Italian ciabatta is in keeping. Use a peppery Tuscan olive oil and make this in the summer when ripe vine tomatoes are plentiful. Because of the simplicity of the ingredients used, it is even more important than usual that they are of the best possible quality.

INGREDIENTS

- 2 stale ciabatta loaves, sliced
- 1 kg / 2 lb fresh plum tomatoes
- 4–6 cloves garlic, crushed to a paste with a little olive oil and sea salt
- 350 ml / 12 fl oz Tuscan olive oil, plus extra for serving
- 4 tbsp balsamic vinegar
- 3 red peppers

- 3 yellow peppers
- 2 fresh red chillies
- 100 g / 4 oz capers in salt, large fresh ones if possible
- 250 g / 8 oz herbed black olives
- large bunch of basil
- sea salt and freshly ground black pepper

METHOD

Place the bread in a large bowl. Skin the tomatoes with a vegetable peeler and then cut them in half. Place a sieve over bowl. Hold the tomato halves over the sieve and scoop out the seeds, allowing the juices to drip through. Set the tomato halves aside. Season the tomato juice with the garlic and some pepper, adding most of the olive oil and balsamic vinegar. Pour this dressing over the bread and toss until it is all absorbed, adding more olive oil if necessary.

Grill the peppers and chillies until charred on all sides (see page 173), then cut peppers into 8 strips and the chillies very finely. Rinse the salt off the capers.

Place some of the soaked bread in a dish, then add some of the other ingredients, then more bread and continue in this fashion until all the ingredients are used up but with the final layer made up of the colourful vegetables. Allow to rest at room temperature for an hour and serve with more olive oil.

GRILLED BABY VEGETABLES

MARINATED IN CHILLI OIL
AND BALSAMIC VINEGAR

These vegetables are so charming you could give them as a gift, layered according to type in an old-fashioned preserving jar. Keep them refrigerated and eat within 3–4 days. Olive oil is just as desirable if you cannot find a chilli oil. Serve on warmed focaccia or ciabatta bread, with a slice of goat's cheese, a few olives and a small mound of perfect rocket.

SERVES
4 – 6

INGREDIENTS

- 250 g / 8 oz baby courgettes, gently scored with a sharp knife
- 100 g / 4 oz sundried tomatoes in oil
- 250 g / 8 oz baby aubergines
- 250 g / 8 oz firm but red and ripe tomatoes, cut in half
- 100 ml / 4 fl oz chilli oil
- 50 ml / 2 fl oz balsamic vinegar
- 2 cloves garlic, chopped
- 1 piece chilli, finely diced
- juice of ½ lime
- sea salt and freshly ground black pepper

METHOD

Wash the vegetables and baste with half the chilli oil and sea salt. Place under a hot grill for 3–4 minutes turning over until they are charred on all sides. Remove from heat. Mix the balsamic vinegar, chopped garlic and chilli, lime juice, salt and pepper and baste all the vegetables.

Thoroughly wash a preserving jar and rinse it out with boiling water. Dry carefully, then add first a layer of courgettes, then one of sundried tomatoes, then one of aubergines, then a second of sundried tomatoes. Complete with a layer of grilled tomatoes, sprinkled with fresh sea salt. Seal and refrigerate. Return to room temperature before serving.

CHICKPEA SALAD

WITH CORIANDER, PAPRIKA, CUMIN AND YOGHURT SAUCE

This is a particularly rich and powerful salad which can form the main course of a cold summer lunch.

SERVES

6

INGREDIENTS

- I kg / 2 lb chickpeas (cooked weight)
- 100 g / 4 oz onions, diced
- 2 spring onions, neatly chopped
- 25 g / I oz parsley, finely chopped
- 25 g / I oz coriander, finely chopped
- I tbsp paprika
- I tbsp cumin
- 2 cloves garlic, finely chopped
- scant juice of half a lemon

- 200 ml / 8 fl oz olive oil
- 2 tbsp tamari
- 500 g / I lb baby spinach
- salt and freshly ground black pepper

FOR THE SAUCE

- 500 ml / I pint plain or Greek yoghurt
- 25 g / I oz coriander, chopped
- I clove garlic, finely chopped

METHOD

Mix all ingredients except the spinach, 2 tbsp of the olive oil and 1 tbsp of the tamari together and allow to marinate for several hours. The salad should look rich and red, the olive oil brilliant with paprika. At the last moment, toss the baby spinach with the reserved oil and tamari, as well as a few squeezes of lemon juice, in another bowl. Mix the sauce ingredients together.

Heap the spinach loosely onto a plate and spoon the chickpea salad on top with the yoghurt sauce served separately.

NEW POTATO AND GREEN BEAN SALAD
WITH RED ONION AND CHEDDAR CHEESE

Simple to prepare, this salad is a summer meal, complete in itself. Use the smallest new potatoes available so you can leave them whole. As is often the case, this salad is better when left to sit for a while to allow the potatoes to absorb the dressing ingredients. The green beans, however, should be tossed in at the last minute to avoid being discoloured by the balsamic vinegar.

SERVES
6

INGREDIENTS

- 500 g / 1 lb small new potatoes
- 250 g / 8 oz green beans, trimmed
- 100 g / 4 oz red onions, sliced
- 100 g / 4 oz black olives
- 3–4 pieces sundried tomatoes in oil, cut into thin slivers
- 125 g / 5 oz Cheddar cheese, cut into cubes

FOR THE DRESSING

- 1 tbsp grain mustard
- 100 ml / 4 fl oz olive oil
- 1 tbsp balsamic vinegar
- 1 clove garlic, crushed
- salt and freshly ground black pepper

METHOD

Place the potatoes in a pan of salted boiling water and boil for about 14 minutes or until the potatoes are tender. Bring another pan of salted water to the boil and blanch the green beans for 2–3 minutes, then drain and refresh under cold water.

Place the warm potatoes in a bowl and add the sliced red onion, olives and sundried tomato slivers. Finally mix all the dressing ingredients in a small bowl, season and add to the potato salad. Toss in the green beans and cheddar just before serving.

SPROUTED PULSE AND SEED SALAD

WITH GARLIC AND TOFU MAYONNAISE

You might expect to find a salad of this ilk in a health food manual, but if you can put your prejudices aside, you will find that as well as being supremely nutritious, it is also extremely delicious. The tofu mayonnaise is more than you will need but it is so delicious that you should make a large batch while you're at it (it will keep for a few days in the fridge), or simply make only half the recipe if you intend to use it for this salad alone.

SERVES

6

INGREDIENTS

- 25 g / 1 oz pumpkin seeds, dry roasted
- 250 g / 8 oz sprouts, a mixture of mung and lentil
- 2 whole spring onions, finely sliced
- ½ avocado, cut into cubes
- 1 carrot, peeled and cut into thin rings (optional)
- 1 sheet nori seaweed
- 1 level tbsp nori flakes
- large handful of fresh coriander, leaves taken off the stalks

FOR THE DRESSING

- 150 g / 6 oz tofu
- 50 ml / 2 fl oz olive oil
- 150 ml / 6 fl oz water
- 1 tbsp tamari
- 1 tsp Tabasco
- 2 cloves garlic, crushed
- juice of half a lime
- salt and freshly ground black pepper

METHOD

Dry-roast the pumpkin seeds in a pan set over a high flame with salt but no additional oil.

Mix all the salad ingredients except the seaweed, nori flakes and coriander together and set aside. Blend the dressing ingredients until absolutely smooth. Add half of the dressing to the salad and mix well. Place a sheet of seaweed onto a plate, pile on the salad in a mound and garnish with the nori flakes and the coriander.

MIXED BEAN SALAD

WITH CORIANDER SAUCE AND GRILLED
RED PEPPER

The association of beans and pulses with vegetarian food has not always been a happy one but this colourful and delicious salad should change a few minds. Tinned kidney beans are perfect with their glistening skins but I do prefer to cook my own chickpeas and haricot beans.

INGREDIENTS

- 200 g / 7 oz kidney beans, cooked weight
- 200 g / 7 oz haricot beans, cooked weight
- 200 g / 7 oz chickpeas, cooked weight
- 1 bay leaf
- 1 clove garlic, peeled and halved
- 200 g / 7 oz green beans, trimmed
- 1 red pepper, grilled, skinned and cut into slivers (see page 173)
- 1 red onion, finely chopped

FOR THE DRESSING

- 50 ml / 2 fl oz double cream
- 1 tbsp mayonnaise
- juice of half a lemon
- 3 tbsp coconut milk
- 2 cloves garlic, crushed
- small handful fresh coriander leaves
- salt and freshly ground black pepper

METHOD

If you are using dried beans, soak them overnight, keeping each kind separate. The next day, drain them, place in a saucepan, cover with cold water, add the bay leaf and one garlic clove, peeled and halved. Bring to the boil, then reduce the heat and simmer for $1^{1}/_{2}$ hours, until the beans are tender. Drain and set aside.

Cook the green beans in a pan of salted boiling water until just tender but still slightly firm. Immediately refresh under cold water and set aside.

Make the dressing by mixing the cream, mayonnaise, lemon juice and coconut milk until well amalgamated. Add the crushed garlic and season with salt and pepper. Mix in with the beans until well coated. Allow to sit for a few minutes before mixing in the green beans until well coated and at the final moment, the red pepper slivers, the fresh coriander and the chopped red onion. Serve warm or cold.

ROCKET SALAD

WITH PARMESAN AND ASPARAGUS

This is the kind of salad that is perfect as an easy starter or can replace a vegetable dish for a summer meal. I love asparagus – white or green, thick-stemmed or thin, English or otherwise, in season or not. Rocket sown in spring grows profusely all summer long, making the small overpriced supermarket packets looks ridiculous. It has a more peppery taste and, by growing it yourself, you can afford to pile it onto plates in mounds. All bitter leaves are served well by mustard, especially grain, which is a natural companion for the asparagus too.

SERVES

6

INGREDIENTS

- 500 g / 1 lb asparagus, trimmed
- 5 tbsp olive oil
- 1 tsp grain mustard
- 1 scant tbsp balsamic vinegar
- 1 clove garlic, crushed
- 250 g / 8 oz rocket
- 100 g / 4 oz fresh Parmesan cheese
- salt and freshly ground black pepper

METHOD

Peel the stems of the asparagus if necessary. Bring a pan of salted water to the boil and blanch the asparagus for 1–2 minutes, depending on its size. Meanwhile, quickly combine the oil, mustard, balsamic vinegar, crushed garlic and salt and pepper. Immediately pour over the warm asparagus and toss into the rocket. Top with fine shavings of fresh Parmesan and serve at once.

AVOCADO WITH MIXED LEAVES AND PESTO

Another simple, rich salad which makes a delicious starter served with chunks of flat oily Arabic bread or focaccia. Hass avocados are invariably the best with a richer texture but you should still always buy one more than you need because it's practically impossible to guarantee that you won't land on one with blackened flesh.

INGREDIENTS

- 2 avocados, peeled and cut into even-sized 2.5 cm / 1 in chunks
- 150 g / 6 oz mixed lettuce leaves, preferably very young

FOR THE DRESSING

- 75 g / 3 oz good quality pesto
- 50 ml / 2 fl oz olive oil
- salt and freshly ground black pepper

METHOD

Mix the dressing ingredients together and then toss with the avocado. Mix with the lettuce leaves and serve at once.

CHICORY, WATERCRESS AND POMEGRANATE SALAD

WITH WALNUT OIL

The pomegranate seeds in this salad look like jewels. Be sure to pick a pomegranate with bright smooth, deeply coloured skin. Pomegranate and sesame seeds are used to herald in the Jewish New Year and are a symbol of bounty and fecundity. Squeezing the juice from the pomegranate is a messy business but good fun!

SERVES
4 – 6

INGREDIENTS

- 1 pomegranate
- 150 g / 6 oz watercress
- 2 heads chicory, outer leaves removed and chopped

- 1 tbsp walnut oil
- 1 tbsp sesame seeds, lightly toasted
- freshly ground black pepper

METHOD

Cut off a third from the pomegranate and set aside. Remove the seeds from the remaining two-thirds. Mix the seeds together with the watercress and chicory. Then squeeze the juice from the remaining pomegranate into the walnut oil and mix. Pour all over the salad, sprinkle with freshly ground black pepper and sesame seeds and serve at once.

NEW POTATO SALAD

WITH HERBS AND PARMESAN

Potato salads are invariably best served warm so the dressing is more readily absorbed. But forget stodgy potato mayonnaise and try an olive oil dressing, rich with fresh herbs, garlic and Parmesan. The salad can form a base for other ingredients such as spinach or rocket which will wilt in the heat, or a few wild mushrooms, cut into slivers, sautéed briefly and thrown in. Potatoes love onion, so very finely chopped, almost minced red onion will go beautifully. Green beans are another successful addition and the Parmesan can be replaced by another strong-tasting cheese, such as Pecorino.

SERVES

6

INGREDIENTS

- 1 kg / 2 lb new potatoes, cut in half if large
- 1–2 cloves garlic, crushed
- 125 ml / 5 fl oz olive oil
- 1 bunch of chives, finely snipped
- 1 tsp fresh thyme or other herb of your choice, chopped
- 1 tsp fresh chervil or basil, chopped
- 75 g / 3 oz Parmesan cheese, thinly shaved
- sea salt crystals and freshly ground black pepper

METHOD

Place the potatoes in a large pan of salted water and bring to the boil. Cook for 10–15 minutes or until the potatoes are tender. Drain and set aside. Meanwhile, mix the finely crushed garlic with the olive oil and salt and pepper. Mix this and the fresh herbs with the potatoes while they are still warm and finally, just before serving, top with the shavings of Parmesan.

KOHLRABI AND PEAR
WITH A DOLCELATTE DRESSING
AND FRESH WALNUTS

This is an unusual salad which requires pears at the very peak of perfection. William pears are the best, especially when their skins are lightly tinged with orange. I use Dolcelatte because it is the mildest and creamiest of blue cheeses and goes beautifully with walnuts. Use wet, fresh walnuts when they are available at the start of their season in the early autumn, but whatever you do, don't use those rancid-tasting and often bitter pre-packed walnuts.

SERVES
6

INGREDIENTS

- 2 kohlrabi, peeled and sliced practically paper-thin
- I avocado, peeled and cut into thin slices
- 4 perfect William pears, cored and sliced into thin segments
- 3 walnuts, shelled and roughly chopped

FOR THE DRESSING

- 100 g / 4 oz Dolcelatte
- 150 ml / 6 fl oz smetana or sour cream
- I–2 tbsp warm water
- freshly ground black pepper

METHOD

Bring a pan of salted water to the boil and plunge the slices of kohlrabi into it for 10 seconds. Drain thoroughly.

Assemble each serving separately in concentric rings, starting with kohlrabi slices, then avocado slices and finishing off with pear slices.

To make the dressing, blend the Dolcelatte with the smetana and the warm water to make a dressing that pours easily. Drizzle all over the salad and complete by scattering the chopped walnuts and freshly ground black pepper over and around the salad.

CHERRY TOMATOES, BLACK OLIVES, BABY CUCUMBER AND BABY MOZZARELLA

A dead easy salad which looks dead good! Baby cucumbers are often available from Greek grocers. They are much sweeter than the larger, polythene-wrapped variety. If you want to make this in advance, add the cucumber only at the last minute.

INGREDIENTS

- 125 ml / 5 fl oz olive oil
- 1 tbsp balsamic vinegar
- 1 clove garlic, crushed
- 125 g / 5 oz baby Mozzarella cheese or 1 large ball cut into chunks
- 500 g / 1 lb cherry tomatoes
- handful fresh basil leaves, purple or green
- 25 g / 1 oz sundried tomatoes in oil, finely sliced
- 100 g / 4 oz mixed green and black herb olives
- 250 g / 8 oz baby cucumber (about 3), peeled and cut into 1 cm / ½ in chunks
- salt and freshly ground black pepper

METHOD

Mix the olive oil with the balsamic vinegar, garlic and salt and pepper and then marinate the Mozzarella for 10 minutes. Mix with the tomatoes, basil, sundried tomatoes, olives and chopped cucumber and serve with warm bread.

BEETROOT SALAD

WITH RED ONION AND BALSAMIC VINEGAR

Three strong red flavours for a simple salad. I know someone
who went on a beetroot fast for several weeks. It's not what
I recommend you do, but on this salad I'd be tempted.

SERVES
6

INGREDIENTS

- 750 g / 1½ lb cooked beetroot
- 1 tbsp almond or sunflower oil
- 1 tsp grain mustard
- 6 tbsp balsamic vinegar
- dash of Tabasco
- 1 tsp caraway seeds, pounded with a little oil in a
  pestle and mortar

- 1 small bunch flat leaf parsley or coriander,
  coarsely chopped
- 2 red onions, diced very small
- 75 g / 3 oz Feta cheese
- coarse sea salt and freshly ground black pepper

METHOD

Cut the beetroot into slices 2.5 mm / ⅛ in thick or into 1 cm / ½ in dice. Mix the oil,
mustard, vinegar, Tabasco and caraway seeds into a thin dressing. Pour over the beetroot
and set aside for at least half an hour to allow the flavours to mingle and develop.

Just before serving, mix in the fresh parsley or coriander (reserving a little for the
garnish), the red onion and finally the coarse sea salt. Pour out onto a plate and
crumble the Feta cheese all over the top. Finish off with the remaining herbs and a
little coarsely ground black pepper.

GRILLED AUBERGINE
WITH SMOKED MOZZARELLA FRITTERS
AND TOMATOES

Jenny Wright, who used to work at Cranks, mentioned the combination of aubergine and smoked Mozzarella to me and I could not get it out of my mind until I made this recipe. You will probably have to order the smoked Mozzarella from a specialist cheese shop, although Italian delicatessens often stock it.

SERVES
6

INGREDIENTS

- 2 medium aubergines, cut into 5 mm / ¼ in slices
- 5 tbsp olive oil
- 500 g / 1 lb good firm, bright red tomatoes
- several leaves basil, finely shredded, plus extra for garnish
- 75 g / 3 oz toasted breadcrumbs
- 3 eggs, size 3, beaten
- 1 litre / 2 pints sunflower oil for deep frying

- 150 g / 6 oz smoked Mozzarella cheese, cut into 5 mm / ¼ in slices
- 150 g / 6 oz rocket

FOR THE DRESSING

- 1 heaped tbsp grain mustard
- 2 tbsp balsamic vinegar
- 125 ml / 5 fl oz olive oil
- freshly ground black pepper

METHOD

Brush the aubergine slices with olive oil on one side and place under a hot grill for 5 minutes. Turn over, brush the other side with olive oil and repeat. Allow to cool slightly, then cut into strips and set aside. Slice the tomatoes and set aside. Make the dressing by whisking the mustard with the vinegar and adding the olive oil and pepper.

Mix the shredded basil and breadcrumbs in a shallow dish. Put the eggs in another shallow dish. Heat the sunflower oil until very hot and then turn the heat down. Dip the Mozzarella slices in the beaten egg and then in the breadcrumbs. Drop gently into the hot oil and turn over quickly to lightly brown both sides – about 20–30 seconds. Remove with a slotted spoon and place on a plate lined with kitchen paper.

To serve, pile a mound of rocket onto each plate, add tomato slices all the way round. Place the fried Mozzarella on top and scatter generously with the strips of fried aubergine. Drizzle the dressing all over. Serve immediately, garnished with a few small basil leaves.

CHINESE LEAF SALAD

WITH WALNUTS AND
CHEESE IN LIGHT MAYONNAISE

This combination of ingredients is irresistible and rather like a sophisticated version of coleslaw. Serve it straightaway and don't let it sit around or it will lose all its appealing crunch.

SERVES
4 – 6

INGREDIENTS

- 1 Chinese leaf
- 100 g / 4 oz mature Cheddar cheese, cut into cubes
- 50 g / 2 oz walnuts, shelled
- 100 ml / 4 fl oz yoghurt
- 100 ml / 4 fl oz mayonnaise
- 125 g / 5 oz watercress
- salt and freshly ground black pepper

METHOD

Remove the outer leaves of the Chinese leaf and discard. Chop the rest and mix with the Cheddar and walnuts. Mix the yoghurt and mayonnaise and pour over the Chinese leaf, Cheddar and walnuts. Serve on a bed of watercress, sprinkled with black pepper.

WARM MUSHROOM SALAD
WITH QUAILS' EGGS

A warm salad cooked in the briefest time, and quails' eggs with egg yolks still soft in the middle. Work carefully to remove the fine shells, using a small sharp knife to cut through the shell and inner membrane. If you are making this as a starter for a dinner party, serve it on tender, young frisée leaves.

INGREDIENTS

- 18–24 quails' eggs
- 4 tbsp olive oil
- 1 kg / 2 lb mixed wild mushrooms
- 2 cloves garlic, finely chopped
- 1 tbsp brandy
- 1 tsp tamari
- 1 tbsp finely shredded basil
- salt and freshly ground black pepper

METHOD

To cook the quails' eggs, boil for $2^1/_2$ minutes and then plunge them into cold water. Cut one open to check that it is cooked. Peel immediately under cold, running water and set aside.

Heat the oil gently in a frying pan and sauté the mushrooms with the garlic, brandy, tamari and salt and pepper for 3–4 minutes. Transfer to a plate and arrange the quails' eggs, cut in half, over the salad. Garnish with the finely shredded basil and serve.

WARM PASTA SALAD

WITH ROCKET, BLACK OLIVES
AND SUNDRIED TOMATOES

Warm pasta salads are delicious when eaten more or less as
soon as they have been made. Add a few Parmesan shavings
to each serving and a small mount of perfect rocket leaves
for a salad that is as pretty as it is delicious. I leave the shape
of the pasta to your imagination and the ingenuity of modern
pasta manufacturers.

INGREDIENTS

- 100 ml / 4 fl oz olive oil or oil that the tomatoes
  have been marinating in
- 500 g / 1 lb pasta shapes
- 2–3 cloves garlic, crushed to a paste with a little
  sea salt
- 1 tbsp balsamic vinegar (optional)
  dash of Tabasco
- 100 g / 4 oz Provençal black olives

- 100 g / 4 oz sundried tomatoes in oil,
  cut in slivers
- 50 g / 2 oz toasted pine nuts
- 1 large bunch basil, leaves only
- 150 g / 6 oz rocket
- 50 g / 2 oz fresh Parmesan cheese
- salt and freshly ground black pepper

METHOD

Bring a large pan of salted water to the boil. Add a spoonful of olive oil and the pasta.
Cook according to packet instructions. Drain and run briefly under cold water to
prevent the pasta sticking together.

Meanwhile, mix the remaining olive oil with the garlic paste, balsamic vinegar,
Tabasco and salt and pepper to taste. Pour over the warm pasta and mix with the olives,
sundried tomatoes, pine nuts, basil and half the rocket so that it just begins to wilt in
the remaining warmth. Reserve the rest of the rocket to pile into light and pretty
mounds on top of each plate. Finish off with several shavings of Parmesan.

CAULIFLOWER AND BROCCOLI SALAD

WITH ROASTED RED PEPPERS AND GRAIN MUSTARD DRESSING

This dressing can be as bold as you dare but save it for the weekend or drastically reduce the garlic count! The longer you can allow the cauliflower to marinate in the garlic dressing, the better. I rarely resist the temptation to add olives to this salad, but then I rarely resist the temptation to add olives to anything, so they are not included in the ingredients but are left up to you. Cauliflower can take quantities of grain mustard so go as far as you wish.

SERVES

6

INGREDIENTS

- 1 large cauliflower, outer leaves and stalk removed and separated into florets
- 500 g / 1 lb broccoli, separated into florets
- 2 red peppers, chargrilled, peeled and thinly sliced (see page 173)

FOR THE DRESSING

- 100 ml / 4 fl oz extra-virgin olive oil
- 1 heaped tbsp grain mustard
- 15 g / ½ oz fresh tarragon, picked off the stalks
- 4 cloves garlic, finely crushed
- dash of Tabasco
- dash of balsamic vinegar
- salt and freshly ground black pepper

METHOD

Plunge the cauliflower and broccoli florets into a pan of salted boiling water and blanch for 1 minute until tender but still firm. Meanwhile combine the dressing ingredients. Combine all the salad ingredients in a bowl and pour over the dressing while the cauliflower and broccoli are still hot. Add more grain mustard to taste if necessary. Add olives if using, and serve with a simple couscous salad or warm pasta bows, or as part of a combined salad plate.

desserts

There are some people who feel that a meal isn't complete without a proper pudding with lashings of cream or, at the very least, a light, fruity dessert. In this chapter, you'll find something to suit you, whatever your preference.

have it easily at hand. Draw a circle 20 cm / 8 in in diameter, using an upturned plate or cake tin as a guide, on 3 separate pieces of baking parchment. Cut out, lightly brush with oil and set aside.

Begin by whisking the egg whites at a gentle speed so they break down completely and then turn to the fastest speed until they stand in stiff peaks. Immediately add 1 tbsp of the caster sugar until it is thoroughly whisked in and then slowly and spoon by spoon, add the rest of the sugar, mixed with the cornflour. It is essential that each spoonful is well incorporated before you add an other. I count 10 seconds between each spoonful.

Cover one circle of paper with a third of this plain meringue, using a tablespoon to lift the mixture onto the paper and then lightly swirl around with a clean skewer or tines of a fork. Add the coarsely chopped nuts to the remaining meringue mixture and spread over the last two pieces of paper as before. Place in a preheated (albeit very low heat) oven and allow it to dry out for 1 hour. Remove from oven. Turn upside down onto a large flat plate and carefully peel off the paper.

While the meringue is in the oven, make the chocolate mousse. Whisk the cream, adding the icing sugar until it just holds stiff peaks. Set aside. Place the softened butter, cocoa powder and caster sugar in a large mixer bowl. Add the egg yolks and brandy and whisk slowly at first as otherwise the cocoa powder will rise in a cloud. When mixed in, gather up speed and continue to whisk for several minutes until the mixture is smooth and voluminous and there is no trace of powderiness. Fold in the sweetened whipped cream and set aside.

Make the Chantilly by whisking the cream and sugar together.

To assemble, place on circle of almond meringue, smooth side up, on a large flat plate. Spread carefully with half the chocolate mousse, taking the mixture up to the edges but thinly enough so that it does not spill out when you add the next layer. Then cover with a layer of plain meringue, a second layer of chocolate mousse and a layer of Chantilly on top of that, finally a second and last layer of almond meringue. Serve at once.

Both the meringue and chocolate mousse freeze very well. The chocolate mousse will have to be thawed out first but the meringue can be used straight from the freezer. Alternatively, freeze the assembled dessert and eat it while it is still very cold.

COCONUT, CARDAMOM AND LIME ICE CREAM

You could substitute ordinary milk for the coconut milk and replace the cardamom seeds with a vanilla pod to make a simpler ice cream if you wish. Either way, this ice cream is excellent served with the Pumpkin Pie on page 251.

SERVES
6

INGREDIENTS

- 250 ml / 10 fl oz coconut milk
- 250 ml / 10 fl oz double cream
- zest of 1 lime

- ½ tsp cardamom seeds, crushed
- 200 g / 7 oz caster sugar
- 6 egg yolks

METHOD

Place the coconut milk, double cream, lime zest, cardamom seeds and half the sugar in a saucepan and bring to the boil, then immediately remove from heat. Cream the egg yolks with the remaining sugar in a separate bowl, then pour the hot mixture into them, stirring all the time. Return this mixture to the pan and heat over a very low heat, stirring constantly with a wooden spoon, until the custard is thick enough to coat the back of the spoon. The custard must on no account be allowed to boil.

Strain the custard through a fine sieve and set aside to cool. Finally, pout the cooled mixture into a plastic bowl and place in the freezer.

About 30 minutes later, when the ice cream is beginning to set, remove from the freezer and beat thoroughly with an electric hand whisk to break down any ice crystals that may have formed. Repeat this process two or three times until the ice cream is completely set. The whole process takes 2–3 hours.

EXOTIC FRUIT SALAD
IN A RASPBERRY SAUCE
SERVED IN A CHOCOLATE BOWL

This is the queen of fruit salads. The raspberry sauce should be thick and as bright as possible with all the tiny seeds sieved out. Use this or another combination of fresh fruit.

SERVES
8

INGREDIENTS

- 2 ripe but still firm nectarines
- 3 or 4 ripe but still firm apricots
- 1 ripe mango
- 1 ripe papaya or pawpaw
- 1 charentais melon
- 3 ripe passion fruit
- 125 g / 5 oz bright red strawberries
- 100 g / 4 oz blueberries or blackberries
- 100 g / 4 oz Chinese gooseberries
- 100 g / 4 oz black cherries

FOR THE SAUCE

- 250 g / 8 oz frozen raspberries, blended and sieved
- 50 g / 2 oz caster sugar

FOR THE CHOCOLATE BOWL

- 250 g / 8 oz good quality dark chocolate
- 1 tbsp almond or sunflower oil

TO SERVE

- 500 ml / 1 pint double or whipping cream or crème fraîche

METHOD

To make the chocolate bowl, break the chocolate into pieces and place in a bowl set over a pan of boiling water until melted. Line a 25 cm / 10 in plastic bowl with foil, pressing it down firmly all the way round. Very lightly brush with the almond or sunflower oil. Use a pastry brush to paint a layer of chocolate onto the foil, making sure it is well covered. Freeze until set and repeat twice more until all the chocolate is used up.

For the fruit salad, carefully wash all the fruit. Remove all seeds and stones from the apricots, nectarines, mango and papaya. Cut into neat 2.5 cm / 1 in squares or use a melon baller on the melon and papaya. Scoop out the seeds from the passion fruit and slice the strawberries if they are large. Mix all the fruit together.

To make the raspberry sauce, place the raspberries and sugar in a liquidizer and blend until smooth. Pass through a fine sieve to remove all the seeds – this is essential. Mix into the fruit salad. Just before serving, ease the foil-covered chocolate bowl from the plastic bowl and carefully peel off the foil. Place the chocolate bowl on a large serving plate and fill with fruit salad. Serve with whipped cream or crème fraîche.

LEMON TART

This is a particularly lemony and creamy version of a popular and classical dessert. Another version can be made with orange or lime juice and the addition of coconut or split cardamom pods left to infuse in the cream, then strained.

SERVES
8 – 10

INGREDIENTS

FOR THE PASTRY

- 125 g / 5 oz unsalted butter, cut into small pieces
- 25 g / 1 oz caster sugar
- 200 g / 8 oz plain flour, sifted
- ice-cold water

FOR THE FILLING

- 250 ml / 10 fl oz double cream
- juice and zest of 5 lemons
- 4–5 cardamon pods (optional)
- 285 g / 10 oz caster sugar
- 9 eggs, size 3
- 1 tsp icing sugar to garnish

METHOD

For the filling, heat the cream to just boiling point then remove from the heat and infuse with the lemon zest and the cardamom pods, if using, for several hours or preferably overnight. Then, add the caster sugar and beat in the eggs one at a time.

Make the pastry by placing the butter, sugar and flour in a bowl and working lightly with your fingers until the mixture turns to fine crumbs. Bring the pastry together by adding a little ice-cold water. Set aside in the fridge for about 20 minutes.

Preheat the oven to 200°C/400°F/gas 6. Roll out the pastry and line a 25 cm / 10 in round, loose-based tin, reserving a small amount of pastry to patch up any cracks which may appear after it has been first baked. Prick all over with a fork and bake in the preheated oven for 15 minutes or until pale gold.

Allow the pastry case to cool, then pour in the lemon custard and bake for 1–1½ hours at 130°C/250°F/gas ½. Do not allow the top to brown at all. When just set, remove from the oven and allow to cool for a couple of hours. Lightly dust with icing sugar around the edges and serve.

CREME BRULEE

These individual desserts are easy to make, and look stunning topped with caramelized sugar. To put the leftover vanilla pod to good use, leave it to dry out after infusing the milk and then put it in an airtight jar with some caster sugar and you have vanilla sugar to use as you would ordinary sugar, but with a lovely, delicate vanilla scent.

SERVES

8

INGREDIENTS

- 350 g / 12 oz soft brown sugar
- 12–13 egg yolks, size 3
- 100 ml / 4 fl oz milk
- 125 ml / 5 fl oz double cream
- 1 vanilla pod

METHOD

Preheat the oven to 180°C/350°F/gas 4.

Mix half the sugar with the egg yolks in an electric mixer at low speed 2, until thick and creamy. Gently heat the milk and double cream together with the vanilla pod but do not boil. Remove the vanilla pod, wipe clean and keep. With the mixer turned even lower to speed 1, gradually add the milk and cream to the beaten egg and sugar.

Pour the mixture into individual ramekins and place in a bain marie one-third full of water. Bake in the preheated oven for about 1 hour, or until just set. Remove and chill straight away.

When ready to serve, sprinkle the rest of the sugar evenly over the surface and caramelize under a very hot grill, watching it carefully to make sure it does not burn. Serve as soon as the sugar has hardened.

BAKED WINTER FRUIT

This is a sugar-free, guilt-free dessert that is nonetheless delicious and warming. It is also very simple to make and therefore ideal for when you are entertaining because it can be left to bake slowly in the oven while you attend to the rest of the meal. Don't bother with cooking apples, but do choose fruit with as much flavour as possible. You could, of course, add brown sugar if you like, sprinkled on at the end, just before going under the grill, where it will caramelize beautifully.

SERVES

6

INGREDIENTS

- 3 Cox's apples, large
- 3 pears, preferably Comice, just ripe
- 18 prunes, ready stoned
- 12–18 figs, dried but moist
- 18 soft dried apricots
- 1 orange

- 100 ml / 4 fl oz apple juice
- 1 small piece ginger, finely grated
- pinch of cinnamon
- 25 g / 1 oz flaked almonds, toasted
- zest of 1 lime
- Greek yoghurt, for serving

METHOD

Preheat the oven to 180°C/350°F/gas 4.

Cut the unpeeled apples and pears into quarters, first removing the cores. Place in a large shallow glass or other ovenproof dish and add the prunes, figs and apricots. Remove the orange peel with a zester and set aside. Squeeze the juice over the fruit and mix with the apple juice, ginger and cinnamon. Cover with foil and place in the preheated oven for 1 hour.

When baked, remove the foil, stir the fruit around so it is well coated with juice and place the dish under a hot grill for a couple of minutes, so that the fruit just slightly chars in places. Garnish with the toasted flaked almonds and orange and lime zest, reserving some of each to garnish the Greek yoghurt. Serve hot or cold.

PINEAPPLE, RAISIN AND COCONUT CRUMBLE

Crumble sales at Cranks tripled the week this version appeared on the menu.

SERVES
8 – 10

INGREDIENTS

- 1 kg / 2 lb pineapple (approximately 2 pineapples)
- 25 g / 1 oz raw cane sugar
- 200 g / 8 oz raisins
- 50 g / 2 oz desiccated coconut
- 1 tbsp rum or brandy
- 1 tsp ginger, finely chopped
- 1 quantity crumble mixture (see p 220)
- custard or double cream, for serving

METHOD

Peel and cut the pineapple into even-sized cubes. Place in a pan with all other ingredients except the crumble mixture and simmer gently for 5 minutes.

Preheat the oven to 200°C/400°F/gas 6.

Pour the pineapple mixture into an ovenproof dish and sprinkle generously and loosely with the crumble mixture. Don't press the mixture down or you will lose the desirable crumbly texture and end up with a hard crust instead. Bake in the preheated oven for 35 minutes, or until the crumble is set in large lumps and very pale gold in colour. Serve warm, with custard or double cream.

CHOCOLATE PECAN TART

I love the rich, sticky sweetness of pecan tart and the decadent addition of chocolate makes this a dessert for times when the sugar cravings are running at their highest. Served freshly out of the oven, still warm and with a dollop of home-made ice cream or double cream, this is almost too rich to tackle at the end of a full meal. But reserved for a Sunday afternoon tea time with friends, oh bliss!

SERVES
8 – 10

INGREDIENTS

- 150 g / 6 oz caster sugar
- 85 g / 3½ oz butter
- 2 eggs, size 3, beaten
- 1 tbsp cornflour
- 250 g / 8 oz pecan nuts, halved
- 100 g / 4 oz dark chocolate, broken into small pieces
- 1 tsp cocoa powder, dissolved in 1 tsp cold water
- 1 prebaked sweet pastry case (see page 222)

METHOD

Preheat the oven to 190°C/375°F/gas 5.

Place the sugar and butter in a mixer bowl and beat until light and fluffy. Add the eggs, a little at a time, beating well after each addition. Fold in the cornflour, three-quarters of the pecan nuts, chocolate and cocoa liquid until evenly blended.

Pour the mixture into the prebaked 30 cm / 12 in pastry case and decorate with the remaining pecans. Bake in the preheated oven for 40–45 minutes or until the filling has set. Serve warm with extra thick double cream or crème fraîche.

FRUIT SAVARIN

Savarin dough is very similar to brioche dough but has twice as much milk and half as much butter. It is very lightly sweetened, hence its suitability for desserts like rum babas, when the dough is drenched with sugar syrup, and for this recipe when the finished savarin is soaked through with the juice of mixed berries. In fact the juice needs to be spooned over for a good 10 minutes, so that it is thoroughly absorbed and the savarin becomes moist and bright red. Savarin dough must be used as soon as it is made. Once risen, it cannot be allowed to rest at all.

This recipe is based on one by the Roux Brothers and the poppyseeds were Suzanne Cullen's idea.

SERVES

6

INGREDIENTS

- 15 g / ½ oz fresh yeast
- 200 ml / 8 fl oz warm milk
- 2 tsp salt
- 6 eggs, size 3
- 500 g / 1 lb strong white flour, sifted
- 150 g / 6 oz unsalted butter, softened
- 1 tbsp poppyseeds
- 15 g / ½ oz caster sugar

FOR THE SYRUP

- 350 ml / 12 fl oz water or juice from the frozen berries
- 300 g / 12 oz caster sugar

TO SERVE

- 1 kg / 2 lb frozen mixed berries, especially raspberries or 1 kg / 2 lb mixed fresh blackberries, raspberries and blueberries
- 100 g / 4 oz caster sugar
- 500 ml / 1 pint double or whipping cream, whipped

METHOD

Place the yeast and half the warm milk in a mixer bowl and beat lightly with a wire whisk, then add the salt. Add the flour and eggs and knead the dough using the mixer dough hook for about 10 minutes until it is smooth and quite elastic. Now gradually add the remaining milk to obtain a supple dough which does not break when you stretch it between your fingers.

Place the dough in a bowl covered with a cloth and leave to rise for about 1 hour in a warm place or until it has doubled in volume. Knock the dough back by flipping it backwards and forwards between your hands a couple of times.

Brush the inside of a 25 cm / 10 in ring mould with softened butter and fill with the savarin dough. Rise once more, this time in the tin, for about 40 minutes. Preheat the oven to 200°C/425°F/gas 7 and bake for 30 minutes. Unmould the savarin and return to the oven, placed on a baking tray, for a final 5 minutes so that it is evenly browned all over. Place on a wire rack and allow to cool for 1 hour.

Meanwhile make the syrup by placing the water or fruit juice and the sugar in a pan. Boil for 3 minutes and allow to cool. Place a plate underneath the savarin on the wire rack and spoon the syrup all over, catching the juices as they drip onto the plate and pouring them over again, until the sponge is well soaked.

Place on a serving plate. Mix the berries in the sugar and pile them in the middle and around the top. Pipe a circle of whipped cream around the outer edge. Serve any remaining cream separately.

CHOCOLATE AND WALNUT ROULADE

WITH RASPBERRIES

A festive-looking cake that takes about 30 minute to make
and bake but has all the richness, lightness and sweetness you
could wish for in a dessert

INGREDIENTS

- 500 g / 1 lb dark chocolate
- 2 tsp instant coffee
- 150 ml / 6 fl oz hot water
- 300 g / 10 oz caster sugar
- 10 eggs, size 3, separated
- 1 heaped tbsp coarsely ground walnuts

FOR THE FILLING

- 500 ml / 1 pint double cream
- 250 g / 8 oz fresh or frozen raspberries, defrosted
- icing sugar, to decorate

METHOD

Preheat the oven to 190°C/375°F/gas 5. Line a 30 cm / 12 in baking tray with good quality baking parchment.

Break the chocolate into small pieces and melt in a bowl placed on top of a saucepan of boiling water. Dissolve the coffee in the hot water, add to the melted chocolate and mix well. Remove from heat and set aside to cool.

Meanwhile, whisk the sugar and egg yolks until thick and fluffy so that when the whisk is lifted it leaves behind a trail which holds for a count of 5 seconds. Add the cooled chocolate to the egg and sugar mixture. Then whisk the egg whites until stiff, folding in the ground walnuts so they are evenly distributed in the mixture. Carefully fold the egg whites into the chocolate mixture. Pour into the prepared baking tray and bake in the preheated oven for 12–15 minutes. Check whether the mixture is set by inserting a skewer or the fine point of a knife into the cake and making sure it comes out clean. If not, return to the oven for a further 5 minutes or until set. Leave to cool in the tin.

While the roulade cools, whip the cream. Spread the roulade with the whipped cream, leaving a gap at both ends as it will spread outwards as you roll the roulade, and gently cover with raspberries. Carefully roll up like a Swiss roll, using the paper to help you.

Transfer to a long cake plate and dust with icing sugar. Don't worry if the roulade cracks as you roll it as this adds to its character.

PEAR AND BLACKBERRY CRUMBLE

Another ever-popular crumble.

SERVES

8

INGREDIENTS

CREME ANGLAISE

- 500 ml / 1 pint double cream
- 200 ml / 8 fl oz milk
- 1 vanilla pod
- 5 egg yolks, size 1
- 40 g / 1½ oz caster sugar
- 2 level tsp cornflour

FOR THE CRUMBLE

- 350 g / 12 oz white flour, sifted
- 150 g / 6 oz caster sugar
- 250 g / 8 oz unsalted butter, cubed

FOR THE FILLING

- 1.5 kg / 3 lb pears, ripe but still firm, peeled, cored and cut into 6 slices
- 50 g / 2 oz caster sugar
- 500 g / 1 lb fresh blackberries

METHOD

For the crème anglaise, place the cream and milk in a saucepan with the vanilla pod, bring to a gentle simmer. Remove from the heat and allow the vanilla pod to infuse for 10–15 minutes. Remove the pod and wipe it clean for further use (see page 209).

Meanwhile, whisk the egg yolks, sugar and cornflour together in a bowl, until thick and creamy. Add a little of the hot milk and cream mixture, stir well and return the egg mixture to the pan. Heat again on a gentle heat, whisking continuously until thickened. Immediately remove from the heat and place a piece of greaseproof paper or cling film over the surface to stop a skin forming. Refrigerate until needed.

Make the crumble by mixing the flour and sugar together and add the cubed butter. Rub lightly with your fingers until the mixture turns to soft crumbs.

To make the filling, place the pears and the sugar in a saucepan and cook gently for 8 minutes until softened but still intact. Add the blackberries, stir and remove from heat.

Preheat the oven to 200°C/400°F/gas 6. Place the fruit in an ovenproof dish 30 x 20 cm / 12 x 8 in and cover with the crumble. Bake in the preheated oven for 30–35 minutes until crisped and pale gold. Serve hot with crème anglaise.

LEMON PUDDING

A light and popular lemon dessert often served at Cranks.
Lemon is always a favourite but you could also use other
citrus fruits. Experiment with clementine, grapefruit, lime
and orange juices, alone or in combination.

SERVES

8

INGREDIENTS

- 125 g / 5 oz unsalted butter
- 350 g / 12 oz raw cane sugar
- 6 eggs, size 3, separated
- 100 g / 4 oz white flour, sifted
- rind and juice of 2 lemons
- 800 ml / 1¼ fl oz milk

METHOD

Preheat the oven to 180°C/350°F/gas 4.

Cream the butter with three-quarters of the sugar until smooth and creamy and
doubled in volume. Gradually add the egg yolks with a spoonful of the flour. Beat in
the lemon rind and juice. Fold in the rest of the flour, alternating with the milk. Whisk
the egg whites until stiff, then add the remaining sugar and continue to whisk until
glossy. Carefully fold into the lemon mixture, taking care not to over-whisk or the egg
whites will go flat.

Pour into an ovenproof dish 30 x 20 cm / 12 x 8 in and place in a bain marie. Bake in
the preheated oven for 30–35 minutes until set.

PEAR, ALMOND AND BLACKBERRY TART

If I could only ever eat one dessert again, this would have to be the one.

SERVES
10

INGREDIENTS

FOR THE SWEET PASTRY

- 350 g / 12 oz plain flour, sifted
- pinch of salt
- 200 g / 7 oz unsalted cold butter, diced
- 100 g / 4 oz icing sugar
- 2 egg yolks

FOR THE FILLING

- 250 g / 8 oz unsalted butter, softened
- 250 g / 8 oz caster sugar

- 250 g / 8 oz blanched whole almonds, ground
- 6 eggs, size 3
- 6 ripe Comice pears, peeled, halved and cored
- 150 g / 6 oz blackberries
- crème fraîche or Mascarpone, for serving

TO GLAZE

- 1 tbsp apricot jam, dissolved in a little hot water (optional)

METHOD

To make the pastry, place the sifted flour and salt on a clean, dry surface and make a well in the middle. Put the diced butter in the middle, then work with your fingertips until very soft. Sift the icing sugar onto the butter and work it in until smooth. Add the egg yolks and mix well. Gradually draw in the flour and mix until smooth and amalgamated. Wrap the pastry in cling film and refrigerate for at least 1 hour.

Preheat the oven to 200°C/400°F/gas 6. Butter and flour the sides and bottom of a 30 cm / 12 in loose-based fluted tart tin and roll the pastry on a well floured surface, then lift carefully into place. This may be quite difficult as the pastry is so buttery. Alternatively, simply place the pastry in the tin and press it evenly over the sides and base. Prick all over with a fork and bake blind for 20 minutes until pale gold. Remove from the oven and reduce temperature to 180°C/350°F/gas 4.

For the filling, cream the butter and sugar in a mixer until the mixture is pale and light. Add the ground almonds and blend for a few seconds. Then beat in the eggs one at a time. Place the pear halves face down on the pastry and pour the almond mixture on top, making sure that some of the pear remains exposed. (You can 'fan' out the pears, by making slits in the flesh from top to bottom so they remain attached at one end.) Dot the blackberries evenly all over the surface in between the gaps. Bake for 35–40 minutes or until set. Very lightly brush with the thinned down apricot jam. Serve warm with crème fraîche or Mascarpone.

SUMMER PUDDING

Seasonality not being what it used to be, there is no reason why you shouldn't make this pudding with frozen berries as well as with fresh ones so you can enjoy it all year round. In winter you may like to warm the frozen berries to allow the juices to soak through more easily with no need for overnight refrigeration. You could even sprinkle it with a little extra caster sugar and give the pudding a quick blast under a hot grill. Rolling the slices of bread that are to line the dish with a rolling pin helps them to stay in place. The remaining slices can stay as they are.

SERVES
8 – 10

INGREDIENTS

- 1½ loaves white sliced bread, crusts removed
- 1 kg / 2 lb mixed summer berries
- 250 g / 8 oz soft brown sugar
- mint leaves and cinnamon, to decorate
- crème fraîche or double cream, for serving

METHOD

Line a rectangular 25 x 20 cm / 10 x 8 in ovenproof dish with 10 slices of the bread. Reserve a couple of tablespoons of the berries for decoration (if using fresh) and mix the rest with the sugar. Place one-third of them over the first layer of bread. Add a second layer of sliced bread. Add more berries so that no white shows through. Repeat one more time, finishing off with a layer of bread. Weigh down the bread with another dish or other appropriate weights. Refrigerate overnight weighted down in this fashion, so that all the bread is well soaked through with berries and juice.

Serve with crème fraîche or double cream, lightly sprinkled with cinnamon. Decorate with a couple of fresh mint leaves, and the reserved berries and serve.

BREAD AND BUTTER PUDDING

Much of the culinary revival in British food has been led by the wealth of recipes in the category of sticky, gooey comfort puds. No other country seems to produce these hot, filling, meal-after-a-meal, wicked concoctions. As a child, my mother would refer to them as Les Puddings Anglais and, no matter what they were called, we loved them. The passage of time has not diminished my fondness for them either.

INGREDIENTS

- 50 g / 2 oz butter, plus 25 g / 1 oz for the apples (optional)
- 150 g / 6 oz soft brown sugar, plus 2 tbsp
- 3 dessert apples, peeled and sliced
- 200 g / 7 oz raisins
- 50 ml / 2 fl oz brandy

- 6 eggs, size 3
- 150 ml / 6 fl oz double cream
- 500 ml / 1 pint milk
- ½ tsp cinnamon
- 400 g / 14 oz (8 slices) day-old white bread, crusts left on and sliced

METHOD

Melt 25 g / 1 oz of the butter in a saucepan, add 2 tbsp of the sugar and gently cook the apple slices for 6–7 minutes, or until they are tender. Set aside. Soak the raisins in the brandy for 20 minutes.

Preheat the oven to 180°C/350°F/gas 4. Butter a 25 x 20 cm / 10 x 8 in ovenproof dish. Mix the eggs and the remaining sugar with an electric hand-held mixer and add the cream, milk and most of the cinnamon.

Butter the bread on one side only and cut across into 2 triangles. Place half the bread, butter side up, in the bottom of the ovenproof dish. Then scatter with half the raisins and half the apple and place the remaining bread slices on top. Cut in half and overlap the sandwiches so they are standing almost upright. Scatter with the remaining raisins and apple and pour the egg and cream mixture all over. Sprinkle with a little more cinnamon and 2 tbsp of sugar. Place in the preheated oven and bake for 35 minutes or until the top layer of bread is crunchy and golden and the custard is just set.

If you wish, finish off the pudding by placing under a hot grill for 2 minutes to caramelize the sugar.

cakes and

baking

Cakes are popular teatime treats, and in this chapter you'll find the old favourites like carrot cake and date slices, plus exciting new ideas such as orange parsnip cake, pear tarte tatin and polenta and ricotta cake.

For a very long time all the cakes at Cranks were made with only wholemeal flour. This certainly created a new style of baking, which went some way towards making the health-conscious feel less guilty about eating cakes. Some of these recipes were successful and even seemed to benefit from being made with wholemeal flour – carrot cake is a good example. But, there are definitely some recipes that require the more delicate texture of white flour.

Many of the recipes in this chapter are well suited to afternoon teas, especially in the winter when you feel the need for a comforting slice of something sweet to brighten a dull day. There are also foolproof recipes for baking your own breads, scones and brioche.

Whatever the occasion, eat cake, enjoy to your heart's content and never, ever feel even the tiniest bit guilty.

ORANGE PARSNIP CAKE

It may not seem obvious, but it makes perfect sense to use parsnips in a dessert. They are naturally full of sugar and lend themselves as well to baking as their obvious cousin, the carrot of the by now legendary Carrot Cake (see page 238).

SERVES
8

INGREDIENTS

- 1 prebaked sweet pastry case (see page 222)
- 125 g / 5 oz butter, cut into cubes
- 2 tsp grated orange rind
- 50 g / 2 oz soft brown sugar
- 2 tbsp orange juice

- 3 eggs, size 3
- 65 g / 2½ oz self-raising flour
- 65 g / 2½ oz wholemeal self-raising flour
- 275 g / 9 oz parsnips, peeled and finely grated
- crème fraîche for serving

METHOD

Preheat the oven to 200°C/400°F/gas 6. Cream the butter, orange rind and sugar with an electric hand-held mixer until pale yellow. Add the orange juice and beat in the eggs, one at a time. Fold in the flours and grated parsnip. Pour the mixture into the pre-baked pastry case and bake in the preheated oven for 1 hour or until firm to the touch. Serve with crème fraîche.

CARROT CAKE

Carrot cake is as much a part of the fabric of Cranks as Homity Pie and Cheese Scones (see pages 108 and 246). Try removing any of them from the menu and there is an outcry. Customers threaten never to return and staff are up in arms. Cranks has come a long way but these signature recipes hold an almost hallowed place. The only change you will find in this recipe is the addition of metric measurements.

SERVES
8

INGREDIENTS

- 150 g / 6 oz carrots
- 2 eggs, size 3
- 100 g / 4 oz raw brown sugar
- 5 tbsp sunflower oil
- 100 g / 4 oz wholemeal self-raising flour

- 1 tsp ground cinnamon
- ½ tsp ground nutmeg
- 50 g / 2 oz desiccated coconut
- 50 g / 2 oz raisins

METHOD

Grease and line the base of a 18 cm / 7 in square cake tin. Preheat the oven to 190°C/375°F/gas 5.

Finely grate the carrots. Whisk the eggs and sugar together until thick and creamy. Whisk in the oil slowly, then add the remaining ingredients and mix together to combine evenly. Spoon the mixture into the prepared tin. Level the surface and bake in the preheated oven for 20–25 minutes, until firm to the touch and golden brown. Cool on a wire tray.

POLENTA AND RICOTTA CAKE

WITH APRICOTS AND BRANDY

This is a lovely, easy-to-eat cake made with two typically Italian ingredients. I've added the apricots to lighten the rich texture with a gentle tanginess. The brandy is a wicked note in an otherwise rather virtuous cake.

SERVES
8–10

INGREDIENTS

- 250 g / 8 oz soft, dried apricots, sliced
- 4 tbsp apricot or ordinary brandy
- 200 g / 7 oz polenta (not the instant type)
- 200 g / 7 oz self-raising flour
- 1 rounded tsp baking powder
- 250 g / 8 oz caster sugar
- 250 g / 8 oz very fresh Ricotta cheese
- 100 g / 4 oz butter, melted

- 175 ml / 7 fl oz tepid water
- 50 g / 2 oz walnuts, chopped
- 1 level tbsp demerara sugar
- 1 tbsp apricot jam dissolved in boiling water, to glaze
- 250 g / 8 oz Mascarpone cheese, to serve

METHOD

Place the chopped apricots in a bowl with the brandy and allow the flavours to develop for at least 15 minutes.

Preheat the oven to 170°C/325°F/gas 3. Line a 20 cm / 8 in loose-based tin with baking parchment.

Sift the polenta, flour and baking powder into a large bowl and tip the polenta grains left in the sieve into the bowl. Add the caster sugar, Ricotta, melted butter and water and whisk with an electric hand-held whisk for about 1 minute until well blended. Fold in the nuts, apricots and brandy. Spoon the mixture into the prepared tin and smooth the surface with the back of a spoon. Scatter the demerara sugar evenly over the surface. Bake on the middle shelf of the preheated oven for 1–1¹/₂ hours, or until the cake springs back when gently pressed in the middle. Cover the top with foil for the first 30 minutes.

Leave the baked cake in its tin for 15 minutes, then turn out onto a wire rack and leave to cool completely. Glaze with the apricot jam and serve with the Mascarpone.

PEAR TARTE TATIN

For many years tarte tatin was one thing and one thing only – an upside-down apple pie made famous by the Tatin sisters who invented it. Recently though, the name Tatin has been applied to any and every combination of fruit and vegetables as long as they are baked upside-down and turned out before serving. Pears work really well because of their high sugar content which aids their caramelization. Don't be tempted to use under-ripe pears as no amount of cooking will substitute for their natural sugars and flavours when ripe.

SERVES

8

INGREDIENTS

- 250 g / 8 oz unsalted butter
- 250 g / 8 oz raw cane sugar
- 6 firm, ripe pears, peeled, cored and quartered
- 200 g / 8 oz ready-made puff pastry

METHOD

Preheat the oven to 220°C/425°F/gas 7.

Melt the butter and sugar together in a saucepan over a gentle heat. When they start to caramelize, add the pear quarters. Cook, turning over regularly until the pears start to brown. Place the cooked pears close together and face up in a 20 cm / 8 in cake tin and pour over the excess caramel. Roll out the pastry slightly larger than the tin and place over the pears, tucking in the edges.

Bake in the preheated oven for about 20 minutes or until the pastry is crisp and brown. Serve warm with crème anglaise (see page 220), pouring cream, Mascarpone cheese or pecan ice cream (see page 225).

DATE AND FIG LOG

This is easy to make, good for you and dairy-free. It is delicious as it is, served with an orange and brandy sauce, or use the mixture as a filling for deep-fried sweet wontons (see page 24), served with the same sauce. It is also excellent served with vanilla ice cream. Good quality coconut flakes can be bought from well-stocked health food shops and are preferable to the usual packets of desiccated coconut flakes.

INGREDIENTS

- 250 g / 8 oz dates (Mejdool are best)
- 250 g / 8 oz soft dried figs
- 2 tbsp Marsala wine
- 75 g / 3 oz coconut flakes, two-thirds chopped and the remainder left whole
- 50 g / 2 oz whole almonds, roughly chopped
- ½ tsp fresh grated ginger (optional)

FOR THE SAUCE

- 100 g / 4 oz butter
- 125 g / 5 oz caster sugar
- zest and juice of 3 oranges
- zest and juice of 1 lemon
- 2 tbsp Grand Marnier or Cointreau
- 3 tbsp brandy

METHOD

Stone the dates and remove the stems from the figs. Place on a board and chop vigorously into small pieces. Transfer to a bowl and add the wine, coconut flakes, chopped almonds and ginger, if using. Mix well with your hands and shape into a log.

To make the sauce, place the butter and sugar in a saucepan and melt over a gentle heat. Add the orange and lemon juice and zest and stir for 1 minute. Add the orange liqueur and brandy and continue to simmer for 2–3 minutes.

To serve, cut the log into 1 cm / ½ in slices and dip into the sauce, gently turning until well coated. Serve with a pool of sauce and vanilla ice cream.

The date and fig log can be served immediately or wrap in cling film and refrigerate until needed.

CHOCOLATE CAKE

WITH VIOLET CREME FRAICHE

I sometimes glaze the cake and serve while it is still just warm. If you cannot find violets, garnish with strips of candied orange peel.

SERVES
8 – 10

INGREDIENTS

- 250 g / 8 oz butter, softened
- 250 g / 8 oz caster sugar
- 6 eggs, size 3
- 250 g / 8 oz plain dark chocolate, melted and cooled
- 250 g / 8 oz ground almonds
- 100 g / 4 oz fresh white breadcrumbs

FOR THE ICING

- 150 g / 6 oz dark chocolate, broken into small pieces

- 1 tbsp clear honey
- 75 g / 3 oz butter

FOR THE CREME FRAICHE

- 250 g / 8 oz crème fraîche
- 250 g / 8 oz caster sugar
- 2 egg whites, lightly beaten
- 1 bunch violets

METHOD

Line a 20 cm / 8 in cake tin with baking parchment. Grease with butter and dust lightly with unbleached flour. Preheat the oven to 190°C/375°F/gas 5.

Cut the softened butter into small pieces and place in the bowl of an electric mixer. Add the sugar and beat with a whisk attachment on the highest setting until pale and creamy. Add one egg at a time, waiting for each to be well incorporated before adding the next. Do not be alarmed if this looks curdled, it will come back together again as soon as you pour in the melted chocolate. Slowly add the melted chocolate to the egg and sugar mixture. Slowly fold in the ground almonds and then the fresh breadcrumbs. Pour into the tin and bake for 40–45 minutes, or until firm.

Meanwhile, make the chocolate icing. Melt the broken chocolate, honey and butter in a bowl set over a pan of boiling water. When they have melted, stir well with a metal spoon until smooth. Put the still warm cake on a wire rack set over a plate and pour over the icing. For the crème fraîche, fold 1 tablespoon of caster sugar into the crème fraîche. Then separate the flowerheads from their stems, opening them out gently. Using a fine paint brush, coat each petal on both sides with lightly beaten egg white. Lightly sprinkle caster sugar from a teaspoon so that it sticks to the egg white. Place each flowerhead on a wire rack covered with kitchen paper until the egg white has dried and the sugar hardened. Set aside. Decorate both the cake and the crème fraîche with the crystallized petals. Serve at once.

LEMON, LIME AND POPPYSEED TRICKLE CAKE

This is a combination of two old-time favourites, the lemon cake and the poppyseed cake. You can bake it either in a loaf tin or a square tin but the crucial thing is to drench it in lemon syrup so that it is moist and fragrant with a fine coating of icing on top.

INGREDIENTS

SERVES
10

- 125 g / 5 oz butter, cut into pieces
- 2 tsp lime rind
- 2 tsp lemon rind
- 250 g / 8 oz caster sugar
- 3 eggs, size 3
- 200 g / 7 oz self-raising flour, sifted
- 1 tbsp poppyseeds
- 100 ml / 4 fl oz plain yoghurt

FOR THE SYRUP

- 3 tbsp lime juice
- 3 tbsp lemon juice
- 3 tbsp caster sugar

FOR THE DECORATION

- 3 tbsp sugar
- 2 tbsp lemon rind
- 2 tbsp lime rind

METHOD

Preheat the oven to 180°C/350°F/gas 4. Line a 30 cm / 12 in loaf tin with baking parchment, then butter and flour it.

Place the butter and the lime and lemon rinds in the large mixing bowl of an electric mixer and beat until light and creamy. Add the sugar gradually and beat well after each addition. Beat in the eggs one at a time and mix well. Fold in the flour, poppyseeds and the yoghurt, spoonful by spoonful, alternating between the three. Spoon into the prepared loaf tin and bake in the preheated oven for 30–35 minutes until a skewer inserted into the centre comes out clean. Allow to stand in the tin for about 5 minutes, then turn out onto a wire rack.

To make the syrup, place the juices and the sugar in a pan. Simmer gently and stir continually until the sugar dissolves and then bring to the boil, this time without stirring, and boil for 3 minutes. Make holes all over the top of the cake with a fork and pour the hot syrup over the hot cake. For the decoration melt the sugar in a pan without stirring until the sugar dissolves and begins to go golden brown. Add the lemon and lime rinds and stir until coated and caramelized. Carefully lift out the rinds with a fork and arrange all over the cake.

SCONES

The scones at Cranks are big generous things and we sell about 1500 of them a week. We use an organic wholemeal flour and they are made daily by our night bakers. If you can bear to play around with something so quintessentially English, you could always add some contemporary tidbits. Try dried cherries or cranberries in the sweet scones, or sundried tomatoes, black olives, red onion, or even pumpkin for the cheese scones.

SWEET SCONES

SERVES

6

INGREDIENTS

- 250 g / 8 oz wholemeal self-raising flour, sifted
- pinch of salt
- 75 g / 3 oz butter
- 25 g / 1 oz raw brown sugar
- 75 g / 3 oz sultanas
- 100 ml / 4 fl oz milk

METHOD

Preheat the oven to 220°C/425°F/gas 7.

Place the flour and a pinch of salt into a bowl. Rub in the butter until the mixture resembles fine crumbs. Stir in the sugar and sultanas, then add almost all of the milk to obtain a soft, manageable dough. You may need slightly more or slightly less milk than given. Add more milk if necessary.

Knead the dough on a lightly floured surface, then roll out to about 2 cm / ³/₄ in thick. Use a 7.5 cm / 3 in cutter to stamp out the scones. Place about 2.5 cm / 1 in apart on a lightly greased baking tray and bake in the preheated oven for 10–15 minutes until golden. Cool on a wire tray. Serve with strawberry jam and clotted cream.

CHEESE SCONES

INGREDIENTS

- 500 g / 1 lb wholemeal flour, sifted
- 2 tbsp baking powder
- large pinch of salt
- large pinch of cayenne pepper

- 50 g / 2 oz butter
- 250 g / 8 oz Cheddar cheese, grated
- 300 ml / 10 fl oz milk

METHOD

Preheat the oven to 200°C/400°F/gas 6.

Put the flour, baking powder, salt and cayenne pepper in a bowl. Rub in the butter until the mixture resembles fine crumbs. Stir in most of the cheese and sufficient milk to obtain a soft, easy-to-handle dough. Knead gently, then roll out on a lightly floured surface to a thickness of 2.5 cm / 1 in. Stamp out 7.5 cm / 3 in rounds with a fluted cutter and place on a lightly greased baking tray. Brush with milk and sprinkle with the remaining cheese. Bake in the preheated oven for about 20 minutes until golden. Cool on a wire tray and eat as soon as possible.

BRIOCHE

Brioche is that delicious slightly sweet, light, eggy bread that the French eat for breakfast with café au lait. If you don't possess a brioche tin, a round cake tin will do. Simply line it with greaseproof paper twice as high as the tin. Always use a strong flour when making brioche or other yeasted bread and fresh yeast whenever possible. If you want to mix the dough by hand, triple the mixing times given in the recipe. This is not a recipe to attempt unless you have plenty of time – note the double rising times.

SERVES
6 – 8

INGREDIENTS

- 20 g / ¾ oz fresh yeast
- 5 tbsp warmed milk
- 1 tsp salt
- 400 g / 14 oz self-raising flour
- 3 eggs, size 3

- 75 g / 3 oz butter
- 1 tbsp sugar
- 1 egg yolk, to glaze
- 1 tsp milk, to glaze

METHOD

Whisk the yeast and milk lightly with a wire whisk and add the salt. Put the flour in a mixer bowl and make a well in the centre. Into this break the eggs and add the yeast and milk mixture. Beat with a dough hook for 10 minutes until the dough is elastic.

Soften the butter and beat it with the sugar. Slowly add this to the dough, beating continuously on a low setting. Mix for a further 5 minutes, until the dough looks smooth and feels elastic. Cover with a tea towel and leave in a warm place for 1½ hours, or until the dough has risen to at least twice its original volume. Lightly knead again 5–6 times. Turn the dough out onto a floured surface and shape into a large ball. For a traditional brioche shape, cut off a quarter of the dough. Shape the larger piece into a ball and place in a 1 litre / 2 pint brioche mould. Press a hole in the centre with floured fingertips. Shape the remaining piece like an egg and fit the narrow end into the hole. Beat the egg yolk and milk together and use this to glaze the brioche. Brush over the top, with upward movements, to prevent the glaze from dripping down the sides which will make the brioche stick to the tin.

Leave to rise in a warm place for a further 1½ hours, until almost doubled in size. Lightly glaze once more. Preheat the oven to 230°C/450°F/gas 8 and bake the brioche for 40 minutes, until firm and golden. Unmould instantly and cool on a wire rack.

DUTCH APPLE PIE

I have been making this apple pie for years and like it so much I've never bothered with another. As with all pastry recipes, the secret lies in the short thin pastry base, but roll the dough a bit thicker for the plaited top.

SERVES
8 – 10

INGREDIENTS

- double quantity shortcrust pastry (see page 208)
- 2 kg / 4½ lb fragrant Cox's apples
- 50 g / 2 oz butter
- 250 g / 8 oz soft brown sugar
- pinch of cinnamon
- 1 heaped tbsp apricot jam, mixed with a little boiling water

METHOD

Preheat the oven to 200°C/400°F/gas 6. Make the pastry (see page 208).

Peel and slice the apples no thicker than 5 mm / ¼ in. Melt the butter in a saucepan and add the sugar (reserving 1 tbsp for later use), apple slices and cinnamon. Cook on a low heat for 10–15 minutes until some of the apple has dissolved but most is still intact. Remove from the heat and drain any excess liquid.

Generously butter a 30 cm / 12 in loose-based tin and lightly sprinkle with flour, tapping gently to coat the tin evenly.

Roll out two-thirds of the pastry no thicker than 2.5 mm / ⅛ in. Lift onto a rolling pin and lower into the tin, pressing well into the sides and leaving a 1 cm / ½ in overhang. Prick all over with a fork and bake in the preheated oven for 15 minutes.

Roll out the remaining pastry and cut into 8 strips 1 cm / ½ in wide, making sure the strips are long enough to go across the tin's diameter at its widest point. Also cut one extra long strip to go around the circumference.

Add the cooked apples to the prebaked pastry case. Make a lattice of the pastry, weaving the strips over and under each other. Trim any overhanging pieces and cover the edges with the long strip of pastry. 'Flute' the edge by pinching this strip between your thumb and forefinger. Lightly sprinkle with the reserved brown sugar and bake for 20–25 minutes until golden brown. Immediately glaze with the apricot jam and serve hot or warm with crème fraîche or vanilla ice cream.

CRANKS WHOLEMEAL BREAD

No Cranks cookery book would be complete without a recipe for this wholemeal bread. I know people who will make journeys of great lengths to procure a loaf of it. You may add herbs or seeds to the basic mixture. Do not be alarmed by the absence of kneading in the method – that's how it's meant to be.

MAKES
1 LOAF
OR
6 BAPS

INGREDIENTS

- 15 g / ½ oz fresh yeast
- 1 tsp Barbados sugar
- 250–400 ml / 10–14 fl oz warm water
- 1 tsp sea salt
- 500 g / 1 lb organic wholemeal flour

METHOD

Lightly grease a 900 g / 2 lb loaf tin. Mix the yeast and sugar in a small bowl with 150 ml / 6 fl oz of the warm water. Leave in a warm place for 10 minutes to froth up. Combine the salt and flour on a clean work surface. Add the yeast mixture. Gradually add the rest of the water and mix well with your hands.

Place the dough in the prepared loaf tin. Put the tin in a warm place, cover with a tea towel and allow to rise for about 20 minutes or until the dough is within 1 cm / ½ in of the top of the tin.

Preheat the oven to 200°C/400°F/gas 6 and bake the loaf for 35–40 minutes. Allow to cool for a few minutes and turn out onto a wire rack.

To make baps, roll out the dough thickly on a lightly floured surface and stamp out six 10 cm / 4 in rounds. Place on a baking sheet and brush lightly with milk. Leave in a warm place to rise for 10–15 minutes. Bake at the above temperature for 20–25 minutes. Cool on a wire rack and eat as fresh as possible.

PUMPKIN PIE

I love vegetables that can be used in sweet as well as savoury recipes and pumpkin has always been a favourite. This is best in the autumn when pumpkins are abundant and huge as well as just the deep orange colour that is required. This recipe is lighter than most, an effect achieved by whisking the egg whites and folding them in.

It is delicious served hot, and even more delicious when accompanied by lime and coconut ice cream (see page 205). Double cream is pretty good, too.

SERVES
8 – 10

INGREDIENTS

- 1 prebaked pastry case (see page 208)
- 750 g / 1½ lb pumpkin, peeled
- 350 g / 12 oz caster sugar or soft pale brown sugar
- 6 eggs, size 3, separated
- good pinch of cinnamon
- pinch of freshly grated nutmeg
- 4 cardamom pods, seeds removed and pounded in a pestle and mortar
- 175 ml / 7 fl oz double cream
- 40 g / 1½ oz butter, melted
- 1 tsp cornflour

METHOD

Preheat the oven to 180°C/350°F/gas 4.

Cut the peeled pumpkin into 2.5 cm / 1 in chunks and steam for 10 minutes, or until tender.

Place the sugar, egg yolks and spices in a bowl and mix well. Blend the pumpkin in a liquidizer or mash it with a potato masher until smooth, then add the cream and melted butter. Whisk the egg whites with the cornflour until stiff and carefully fold into the pumpkin mixture. Pour into the pastry case and bake in the preheated oven for 50 minutes, or until set. Serve hot, warm or cold.

PRUNE AND HONEY CAKE

An intensely flavoured cake which has always sold very well at Cranks. You could substitute a fine wholemeal flour for half the white flour if you wish.

SERVES

8

INGREDIENTS

- 3 eggs, size 3
- 200 g / 7 oz soft brown sugar
- 200 ml / 8 fl oz sunflower oil
- 150 ml / 6 fl oz milk
- 275 g / 9 oz white flour, sifted
- ½ tsp bicarbonate of soda
- ½ tsp cinnamon
- pinch of nutmeg

- ½ tsp mixed ground cloves (optional)
- ½ tsp mixed spice
- 250 g / 8 oz prunes, soaked, stoned and chopped
- 2 tbsp Armagnac

FOR THE GLAZE

- 3 tbsp clear honey, lightly warmed

METHOD

Preheat the oven to 190°C/375°F/gas 5. Butter and flour a 20 cm / 8 in cake tin.

Place the eggs and sugar in a mixer bowl and whisk until pale and fluffy. Add the oil and milk and continue to whisk until amalgamated. Now add the flour, bicarbonate of soda and the spices and fold in gently. Lastly, fold in the prunes and Armagnac.

Transfer to the prepared tin and bake in the preheated oven for 45–60 minutes or until a thin skewer inserted in the middle comes out clean. Remove from the oven and leave in the tin for 15 minutes then turn out onto a plate.

Make holes over the top of the cake with a fork. Pour the warmed, runny honey all over the cake and serve warm with whipped cream.

DATE SLICES

Date slices are another faithful Cranks standby, and rumour has it that they're slightly addictive. You can cut them into smaller pieces than the ones served in the restaurants and serve them with tea. We use wholemeal flour but I have made it quite successfully with unbleached white flour. This is a perfect winter dessert with cream. You could also add a peeled, chopped apple to the dates for a lighter filling.

INGREDIENTS

- 500 g / 1 lb dates, stoned
- 200 g / 7 oz butter, cubed
- 300 g / 10 oz wholemeal flour
- 100 – 125 g / 4–5 oz soft brown sugar
- 125 g / 5 oz oats
- 2 tbsp water

METHOD

Steam the dates over a pan of boiling water for 10 minutes until softened, then loosely mash with a fork and set aside. Preheat the oven to 200°C/400°F/gas 6.

Rub the butter into the flour until it resembles fine breadcrumbs and add in the sugar. Add the oats and the water and mix in lightly. Pack half the mixture down tightly into an ovenproof dish or tray and cover with the date mixture. Spoon the remaining oat mixture on top of the dates, so it resembles a rough crumble. Bake in the preheated oven for 30 minutes. Allow to cool or serve warm.

INDEX *Alphabetical listing of recipes is in italic*